Being There

BEING THERE

PETER KEESE

Foreword by Michael B. Curry

RESOURCE *Publications* · Eugene, Oregon

BEING THERE

Resource Publications
An Imprint of Wipf and Stock Publishers
199 W. 8th Ave., Suite 3
Eugene, OR 97401

www.wipfandstock.com

PAPERBACK ISBN: 978-1-6667-3562-8
HARDCOVER ISBN: 978-1-6667-9288-1
EBOOK ISBN: 978-1-6667-9289-8

JANUARY 7, 2022 10:42 AM

To Helen

Contents

Foreword

THIS MIGHT WELL BE, as my friend and author Peter Keese describes it, an "accidental book," but if so it is a very happy accident indeed! This is no primer on Clinical Pastoral Education. As he says at the start, there are some very good how-to guides already out there to read and study. No, turn these pages and you will find *stories* . . . thoughtful and real, some that jump out at you and others that sit with you for a while, but all of them together full of the stuff of life.

You will also be introduced to some memorable individuals, fellow pilgrims on this challenging and sometimes crazy journey on which we all find ourselves. Here are new friends with whom you will have the privilege of walking alongside and getting to know: young and feisty J. Mary Jones, seemingly calm and unruffled Victor, Father Carlos whose pedestal has been taken out from under him. These and others will bring a smile to your face, but they also help you and me wrestle with the question of what happens when we dare to show up. They help us ask what we might learn about ourselves and about life when we truly dare to be present and open.

Peter wisely notes that the CPE process is simple, but not necessarily easy. Likewise, in the stories that follow you just might encounter some fresh truths about life that are simple, but not necessarily easy. And in all of it, you will find Jesus right there, calling you, just like those new friends you are about to meet, to come and see what is waiting just around the corner.

God bless you as you read these stories, and in the process rediscover and deepen your own.

—The Most Rev. Michael B. Curry
Presiding Bishop of The Episcopal Church
and author of *Love is the Way: Holding on to Hope in Troubling Times*

Preface and Acknowledgements

My help has come from so many sources—colleagues, students, clients, and friends, many of whom have offered comments. More importantly from my late wife, Helen; from my children, William and Kate, my grandchildren, and my extended family. I am grateful.

This is an imperfect book written by an imperfect author. I expect I will continue to discover even more flaws than I already perceive both in my conceptualization and my practice of the art of Clinical Supervision. I beg the reader's indulgence. Consider me a fellow pilgrim.

In his well-known poem, *Little Gidding*, T. S. Eliot says "We shall not cease from exploration And the end of all our exploring Will be to arrive where we started And know the place for the first time".

In very brief, here's what I have come to know for the first time and what this book will explore:

There are two distinct but completely complementary aspects to pastoral work, known, perhaps more comprehensively as spiritual care—two which pervade this book. Specifically, in Chapter 28, I note the work of the Chaplain and Pastor as attending to spiritual health, as much to the community as to individuals. In Chapter 30, I focus directly on the absolute necessity in our work for us to "be there", to be with . . . . Referencing verse 5 of Psalm 30, I make this point: joy may—*may*—come in the morning, but you cannot know that in the middle of the night, and you cannot skip that step: you'll have to spend that interminable night weeping.

INTRODUCTION

CLINICAL PASTORAL EDUCATION (CPE) is a peculiar animal. It is an educational process; it values the academy, but it is_not academic; it is the post-academic educational process for Clergy. It happens at the bedside, so to speak—that is, in the clinic – Greek, *klinike*=bedside. (Interestingly, the word "clinical" has come to mean the opposite—it now implies coldly distant; CPE retains the older understanding of being by the bedside, up close and personal.) CPE happens through the *practice*, under supervision, of providing pastoral care. It is a simple but not always easy process: practicing, thinking— alone and with colleagues— about the practice, and then going back to the bedside to practice some more. It is about learning from experience.

About a hundred years ago a few folks noticed how dry academic seminary education was, and how poorly it prepared clergy to actually be with people called parishioners. They pioneered what has become Clinical Pastoral Education.

Several books have been written with the intent of explaining what CPE is. My impression is that some have done a better job than others, but that they're all about describing the various components and at least some of the theory of Clinical Pastoral Education. For example, *How to Get the Most out of Clinical Pastoral Education: a CPE Primer,* by my colleague Gordon Hilsman, is exactly what it says, a clear and very useful recent primer, describing various elements of CPE, the reasons for them, and how they fit together. Readers may find my story telling approach and his more theoretical (though he does use illustrative material) approach to be useful complements.

"The ministry of presence" is a phrase which has gained some popularity recently. 'Showing up' is another popular phrase; both showing up and being present are absolutely essential for ministry to happen, but being there involves much more than showing up. After the pastor gets there—up next to the bedside, what then?

This book about CPE consists mainly of stories about what happens then. My hope is that it will bring the reader beside the chaplain and so convey something of the flavor and feel of the CPE experience, with hints of theory here and there.

Soren Kierkegaard said "life can only be understood backwards, but it must be lived forwards". So I am writing this book, at least in part, because it is the way I come to understand my world and myself in it—my life, in short—as Soren K suggests. I have to start writing to understand what I'm thinking about my practice of forty plus years as a Clinical Pastoral Educator, certified by the Association for Clinical Pastoral Education, Inc. It occurs to me that the very writing of this book is another version of the CPE process of education—it is my continuing to reflect on my practice.

I'm writing this book for at least three potential audiences. I'm hoping that people who are considering whether to enroll in a CPE Program will read this and be encouraged to climb aboard and enjoy the ride. And I'm hoping that my colleagues, particularly those who are beginning the journey toward being certified as Educators will find this helpful. And those colleagues who have been at this for a considerable period of time may find it challenging and may, kindly I hope, challenge me. Finally, I'm hoping that the stories are entertaining enough in themselves that they will appeal to a general audience of people who like a good story.

Many who contemplate engaging in the CPE process these days think of it as primarily aimed at hospital (or other institutional) chaplaincy. It certainly is good preparation for that work, but its aim is the much broader population that includes *anyone—non-ordained or ordained— who wants to increase their ability to minister to others.*

When I first thought about writing this, I intended to focus specifically on CPE, but, along the way, it seems to me to make sense to include a broader range of things I have thought about and written over the years, my notion being that they are related to the way I 'do' CPE.

I have a small following of folks who get occasional writings from me via an email list which built up over a few years. It started as a way to make my sermons more widely available than to the congregation who heard them on Sunday mornings. That was back when I was preaching every Sunday. (Some selected few of them appear in an earlier book which I wrote, *Jesus Has Left the Building.*)

Since I departed from that wonderful little congregation, I have continued to send occasional writings. Here's one I sent out recently:

FOLLOW JESUS

Driving along Highway 100 the other day, we passed a Church of Christ Church building with its sign outside advising us to "Follow Jesus".

Which set me to thinking, "Which Jesus?"

Is it the Jesus with long flowing brown hair, blue eyes, aquiline nose—the 'gentle Jesus meek and mild' of Charles Wesley?

Is it the precocious youngster who holds his own with—and astounds—the scholars in the temple?

Is it the Jesus—same long hair—who angrily throws over tables in the temple court yard?

Is it the Jesus whose attention is primarily on the poor and the oppressed—the phrase some liberation theologians and others use to describe his core characteristic: "he has an option for the poor"?

Is it the miracle worker—some would say "magician"–who heals all manner of people and feeds four or five thousand people with a few loaves of bread and a few fish?

Is it the one who claims to have a kingdom?

Is it the wise, Zen-like master who leaves his followers puzzling over his meaning?

Is it the helpless Jesus who dies at the hand of Roman executioners, crying out to God in despair?

Is it the triumphant Jesus who appears to be alive three days after his execution?

Is it the dead/alive Jesus who is suddenly "taken up" into heaven, no more to be seen?

Is Jesus all of these? Some of these? None of these?

Do we have to decide? To choose? What difference might it make?

Who cares?

Well, I got a good many responses, mostly appreciative. Here are three delightful ones:

1."You forgot to say 'the sexy one who got it on with Mary M.— according to the movie!!'"

2. "There you go, always trying to stir up trouble. It's OUR Jesus, of course. White skinned, cleansed with Dove Body Wash, hair conditioned and styled by Revlon, teeth polished by Colgate, in shining silk robes (by Almy?), New Balance walking shoes, and faintly scented with Armani for Men. He would be welcomed in our homes, our clubs and our churches. He would call some of us by name. Others he would acknowledge with a tilt of his head. He would be a Christian, of course, since that is his brand. He'd probably be an Episcopalian, but would not flaunt it. That is the Jesus we know, expect, and demand. Why would it be any other way?"

3. And somebody reminded me about a hilarious—some would also say "sacrilegious"—brief excerpt from the Movie, *Talladega Nights*, that has Will Farrell, playing a race car driver, saying grace, praying to the Baby Jesus. Others chime in with their images of Jesus, one insisting that Jesus was a *man* with a *beard*; but Will insists that he likes Baby Jesus—"the Christmas Jesus"—the best.

Afterwards, I have thought of one more descriptor that I wish I had included, namely, Jesus the story teller.

I begin this book about my life's work as a particular kind of educator—a Clinical Pastoral Educator, to be exact—with this piece about Jesus for two reasons.

First, the story teller; I'm drawn to the notion of Jesus as a story-teller. I am not the only nor the first to suggest that the best way to convey a meaning, or a truth, is by means of a story. And many folks think that

Jesus may best be understood as a master story teller. One important aspect of storytelling that may not always be fully appreciated is that the teller has to trust the hearer. In this regard, it is most likely that the "explanations" in the Gospel accounts were *not* supplied by Jesus, but by the Gospel's authors. As I will say more than once in what follows, one mantra of Clinical Pastoral Education is "trust the process". Tell the story and trust that the hearer will take the meaning. Sometimes she gets the meaning that you got and that you mean for her to get. Sometimes she will get a meaning that surprises you— "I never thought of that!"; or even one that contradicts what you thought. One important way to think about what our students are doing when they visit patients is just this, they are learning to listen carefully to the story, just as the educator listens carefully to his student.

Second, Jesus has arguably been a central figure in the religious/cultural life of this country for most of its existence, even if it may be true that his centrality is waning in our era. The religious commitment of many CPE students is still Christian, though we have expanded to include Jews and, increasingly, Islamists, Hindus, Buddhists, Humanists, Wiccans, and others. My point is that we still have to do business, as Ministers, with the fact of Jesus. Further, attending to the story means attending to the rich complexity and indefinability—not indescribable, just indefinable— of each human life: CPE, as I believe my stories will illustrate— oh, wait, can I trust you, my reader, to get the meaning? —working with people called learners is a joy precisely because the teacher gets to continue to participate in the rich multifacetedness of each.

So here are some stories from my work as a "Certified Educator, Association for Clinical Pastoral Education". The students are real; and the events are as real as I can recall them. In most cases I've used made-up names and otherwise disguised the identities.

In a way, this is an 'accidental' book. I was the Clinical Educator of a group of students in a Unit that was conducted completely on line (during the pandemic corona virus). I never met these students in the clinic, so to speak. We saw each other on our computer screens. As the Unit was progressing I tried to capture for myself something of each student and his process by writing summary stories about some of our encounters. Many of the stories here began in this way, and, though I include other stories, the stories about the members of that group provided the impetus for the book.

A little more orientation to begin may help. The CPE "program" is structured in terms of "Units", defined as 3 or more students involved in 400 hours total, with 300 at the bedside and 100 in seminars devoted to case conferences and other matters relative to developing pastoral relationships; this group under the supervision of an Educator certified by the ACPE. Most programs in our day are located in general, acute care hospitals; two major reasons are that hospitals provide a locus of concentrated ministry practice; and hospitals (particularly those designated as teaching hospitals) are accustomed to having paid trainees in the various medical and para-medical professions in their midst. The stories will flesh out this brief description.

Chapter 1

Pastor Sam
and the Parallel Process

As I SAID AT the beginning, Clinical Pastoral Education is the post-graduate education for Clergy; it is the post-academic, or para-academic, educational process—in the clinic, through the practice, under supervision, of providing pastoral care. Do it, think about it and then do it again.

Sam is in his early forties, an Episcopalian, doing his seminary education while he is also doing his ministry practice in the "clinic" of his three small contiguous parish churches as assigned by his Bishop in cooperation with the Seminary. I am Sam's Clinical Educator, working with him and four others in a twenty-week Unit of Clinical Pastoral Education. I am certified, and the program is accredited, by the Association for Clinical Pastoral Education, Inc.

As part of his CPE process, I require Sam to present a one page "process note" to me each week. Since he and his peers are adult learners, I leave the subject matter of that note to the discretion of the student— it may be personal, professional, theological, psychological, poetic, prosaic, whatever. That process note, along with case material, typically provides the agenda for our weekly individual conference hour.

Sam had written a poignant note, which he titled "Breaking up is hard to do", about the recent ending of a relationship that had been developing for about a year. She, Monique, initiated the breakup, he said; she complained that he was not meeting all of her needs. "But is it realistic to expect that another human being can ever fulfill every desire someone has?" (asked in what I imagined to be a somewhat aggrieved tone). "I don't think so", answering his own question at the end of his note.

As is my custom, I invited Sam to take charge of the agenda for our meeting: "is the content of that note still at the forefront, or are there other matters?" By this I don't mean to imply that mine is a passive role; he may lead, but I'm an active dance partner.

He did want to talk about that relationship and its ending. His erstwhile girlfriend was a clergy colleague, and she had been a support to him, he said, as he talked with her about his struggle with a "problematic" parish. My ears perked up at his mention of the problematic parish; rightly or wrongly, I chose to pursue that line. That is his clinic. It led us to a fairly extensive exploration of his parish assignment. It seems that the problem was located in the largest of the three churches, and that there was a particular parishioner, Mary, who seemed to be fomenting some discontent, ostensibly centered around the way he had taught a confirmation class to some of the children in that congregation. She had sat in the back of his confirmation class, he said, and then organized a later confrontation by several parishioners. It sounded to me like something of an ambush. I found myself feeling a little sorry for Sam, thinking he was new in pastoral ministry and wondering why his Bishop or his Seminary wasn't more supportive. Then I corrected myself: Sam is right where he needs to be, and this is perfect grist for our educational mill; and my work is with Sam; it is not my business to critique the Bishop or the Seminary. In fact, I had to acknowledge to myself—in order to keep it from contaminating my work with Sam—that I have my own not fully resolved feelings about how the institution (represented by Bishops and Seminaries) sometimes mistreats ministers. (As I will say in more detail later, my temptation to take his side vs. the Bishop is my part in the parallel process.)

In Sam's description, it seems that Mary was ever present in that church—literally, apparently, always present in the building, attending to many tasks—cleaning cooking, secretarial, whatever. As we talked further, it emerged that Mary had suffered a medical trauma some years ago. In Sam's presentation of her, she is a rather angry and needy person.

One of the mantras of us CPE Educators is the term and notion of parallel process: what is happening out there is replicated in what is happening in here. It took me a little while to see that Sam is bringing me two instances of the same theme. It always tickles and delights me to discover again and again that, in that sense, every situation with a student is the same every time and is also always new. It is the re-discovery each time that delights me.

Sam was not deliberately or consciously bringing me *his* neediness. The issue that Sam brings—with Mary and with the friend—is the same one. And it takes some exploratory time—some time to look at the specifics of the situation presented—to see the process once again at work. The issue that emerges is what Pastor Sam can learn about how to deal with neediness—theirs as well as his own.

At this point, we can see Mary's neediness and the friend's neediness. Sam's neediness lurks, is implied, but has not yet fully emerged. So Sam, by bringing it into our consultation hour is making it available and offering us—me with him, and he with them—an opportunity to attend to neediness.

As I write this, I am aware that a hero who is fairly constantly with me is the psychotherapist Irvin Yalom. His book, *Love's Executioner*, in particular, exemplifies a wise and sensitive therapist using his own inner life to help inform him about how to connect with his clients. He doesn't use the term "parallel process", but he describes the same thing in his own way. I'm constantly trying to adapt his style and methods into my work.

And I am aware that, as an educator, psychotherapy is not what I am about in any formal sense; my students have not contracted for that, and I am not formally trained or credentialed for it—notwithstanding that I was credentialed as a "Fellow" with the American Association of Pastoral Counselors[1].

Yet the similarities are quite remarkable between what I do as an educator of pastors, what pastors do in their ministry with individuals, and what psychotherapists do. And it may be humility—appropriate and/or false—that keeps us CPE Educators from claiming our psychotherapeutic

---

1. This Association has now been merged into ACPE

skills; our forebears in CPE were quite skittish about being accused of claiming more than they were entitled to; and even today we carefully deny that we are "doing psychotherapy". But I remind myself that the very term, "psychotherapy", is rooted in two Greek words, *psyche*=soul, and *theraps*=service, so that the original psychotherapists, for good or ill, were the clergy—priests, rabbis, imams.

And by exploring with Sam his own dynamic self-processes we are sharpening his ability to use that self in service to the psyche(s) of his parishioners.

Is it time for me to ask him more directly to reflect on the issue that recurs? Is it mine to tell him that he keeps bringing me neediness?

I think I'll trust the process . . .

So, a few weeks later:

It is still working; neediness is still a theme. But you, the reader, will not be surprised to hear that it is more complex than a one theme song. There's always more.

In our conference today he brings what I recognize—and he knows— is a good, competent piece of pastoral work with "Jane", a parishioner, whom he describes as "a rock"—a very solid, dependable member of the congregation. She calls him to tell him that she has just discovered that she has cancer. He listens carefully and deeply; he is touched, genuinely shocked and dismayed. He doesn't say so directly, but it is clear that Sam depends on her, needs her 'anchoring', and is clearly shaken by her news. As we are concluding our discussion of his work and his feelings, he says, "Discussing this with you has helped me; I needed to talk about it." Parallel to the way he was with her, so I was with him—a listening presence; a need was acknowledged and honored. (Should I have named the parallel? Perhaps, but I was content to live it.)

We move on to his process note. Being able to claim good work when he has done it has long been problematic for him— 'it is not Christian to brag'.

"Where did you learn that?"

Immediately he recalls his meeting with the Diocesan "Discernment Committee" which turned down his first request to begin the ordination process; he was "too full of himself", they said.

Sam is a rich, complex, interesting person. As a young man, he had tried to become a professional wrestler; an injury ended that dream. Later he built log cabins. Baptized Roman Catholic as an infant, he later flirted with other brands, trying Eastern Orthodoxy for a number of years before he found his way into the Episcopal Church. And he has written and published two books having to do with what is often called his "faith journey", a fact that he mentioned to me, sort of in passing. (I later went on line and found them listed by Amazon.)

"Do your peers in this Unit know that?"

"I don't think so; I've not told any of them."

I have to say that I was very glad that we stumbled on this. I reminded him that I had previously told him of my sense about him that he tends to make light of himself. It is something I have puzzled over: what is it about that his message to his colleagues is "don't take me seriously"?

I mean, in a way he is the dominant member of his peer group. He is the first to speak; and he will tolerate a silence for only so long before he speaks up; he takes the lead. And yet . . .

This is a man in his forties; he's been around the block a few times. Admittedly he is in the one down position with the discernment committee; so it would have taken considerable *chutzpa* to challenge them. Perhaps wisely, he didn't challenge.

But he seems still to be living with that rebuke.

Don't take me seriously; and I am reminded of Moses, whose response when he is called to speak up for himself (and, according to the story, for his people), is, "I can't do it; I don't have the ability".

But he could, and he did. So Moses, so Sam.

As the Unit is nearing its end, he brings me—for the third time!!—a conversation with a long-time acquaintance, Irene (who is anything but irenic). Soon came the question I almost always ask, "do you like her?"—another attempt to invite self-reflection in service of enhancing his pastoral skills. I was aware that I distinctly dislike her. Well, he is not at all hesitant to acknowledge that he doesn't like her, either. What a rich conversation that engendered. Sam is working so hard to be the caring, accepting pastor—the non-judgmental presence. We kept pressing in to that. Finally: "I do that because the pastor's job is to be Jesus to people." We did agree, as we talked further, that Jesus could be—and probably was more times than we know—a hardass. What we got to is that Sam doesn't like to be the hardass Jesus—perhaps another aspect of his underclaiming and his neediness.

The cost? Obviously, we can think of Sam [Jesus] and discount him like many Christians have over the centuries—soft, white, long flowing brown hair—gentle Jesus, meek and mild; or we can take him seriously. Sam has some responsibility in this regard, as do I and his peers—this is the CPE process.

Chapter 2

Lou Morrow, Super Man

Lou is a Baptist Pastor, serving a Parish of two to three hundred members in a small southern town.

In spite of an often-furrowed brow and serious demeanor, there is in Lou a delightful and wry sense of humor that peeks out from time to time. He is bright and quick to perceive what is happening. I like Lou; I enjoy him.

He works hard. Always. A consistent theme in our work together is his sense of heavy responsibility. He acknowledges that he is feeling more and more weighed down with the burden of doing all that the Senior Minister has to do. Later in the hour that this story is about, he told me that he used to be "more fun" than he is now.

For the second week in a row, the verbatim account of a pastoral visit that he brings to me is of his visit with Juan, a mid-thirties, sometime attendant at his church. This visit is conducted by telephone, since we are all in the midst of dealing with a coronavirus pandemic by keeping physical distance from one another.

Juan was released from prison last March; he had cashed a bad check, was imprisoned and released; failing to keep to the rules of his probation and running from the police landed him back in prison for another year.

He is living now with his family, working on the family farm, and trying to do right. He is engaged to be married, but there aren't any active wedding plans for now,

My practice is never to have read the verbatim material prior to our meeting; I mean, as much as possible, to experience the encounter through participation in it—with, however, the added benefit that we have the luxury of our then re-viewing it.

One striking feature of the reported visit is how focused Lou is on Juan's anger. As we go back over it, having read it through in dialogue, we both note Lou's persistence; he returns again and again to Juan's anger. Lou is working hard. In the pastoral visit, Juan dutifully answers, but—in my reading of it—without much commitment.

"What were you up to?" I asked Lou.

He said that he felt that he had failed to make much of a connection in the visit the week earlier, and this was his attempt at correcting that lack. He was going to get connected this time! Responsible! Serious! Hard working.

"Why focus on anger?"

Let's step aside for a minute here, while I remind you that one factor always at work is the parallel process. Intellectually, I know it is always operative; yet I am delighted and surprised every time it appears, always through the specifics of the particular encounter and the particular people.

I didn't think anger was it, but I was fishing to see what parallel connection might be there for Lou. But it is always more subtle than that and always surprises when it appears—then to be recognized with "oh, of course".

But at this point we hadn't recognized it. So we continued. I pointed out to Lou that his continuing inquiries about Juan's anger felt to me like he was working *on* Juan and not *with* him. That's when I asked the question I come to every time, "Do you like him".

"Yes", Lou said.

"I don't think Juan got any of this from you", I said, "it didn't show".

8

It was at this point that we talked about how serious Lou is—burdened, always needing to do it all and do it right. He told me about how when he goes somewhere with his wife, he has a task and is laser focused on it, while his wife will take in—and thus enjoy—the whole scene.

Would it have been productive in our work together for me to have confessed my recognition of that and my identification with him in it? Perhaps. But I did not.

As we continued to review his meeting with Juan, I asked him to set aside the anger business for the moment and say what strikes him about what Juan is bringing to him. Of course, he knew: I don't remember quite how he named it, but Lou knew that Juan is feeling guilt about what he has done and is craving forgiveness.

Now we're getting close.

At some point in our hour together, I usually ask the student if there is a connection between his brief process note and the clinical material—verbatim. My students always bring me both; the process note is a one-page document on any topic or area of concern or interest the student has.

Lou didn't think so, but we took a look anyhow.

In it, Lou expressed surprise about how a colleague in this Unit of CPE did not see that his—the colleague's—work with his Parishioner was genuinely helpful; we had examined it in our case conference seminar the day before. "It seemed", he said, "that he expected something of himself that only God could do." He went on to say that he could see the good clearly in his colleague's work, but that he, too, often failed to see the good in his own work.

Burden. Responsibility. Guilt. He had failed to lived up to his responsibility to be a good pastor to Juan.

Juan is feeling very guilty; he has failed to live up to his responsibility; he craves to be forgiven; he doesn't believe forgiveness is possible.

By this point Lou is smiling with recognition. I tell him that I don't like his god. His eyes get big for a moment, but he gets it; I don't need to tell him that I'm talking about his demanding and unforgiving god.

He and Juan worship the same god.

And yet . . .

Lou is rich with tenderness and a depth of understanding. In a recent individual conference, we found our way—I don't remember how—into an exploration of his own family of origin. Maybe it was occasioned by my curiosity about his somewhat cautious leadership style combined with a tendency to take on so much. He recalls his father as a leader— his mother, too, now that he thought about it. Father was a no-nonsense kind of man, whose authority was respected and unquestioned by the men who worked for him. Lou reminded me that his father had died some time ago, having had to retire about ten years prior due to chronic obstructive pulmonary disease. Lou recalls watching his father grow weaker, and how very hard that was—hard in large part, because the role of family leader devolved on to him.

It was a very touching moment; Lou was moved, as was I; we both got teary, and we just sat together, silently, for a little while—this earnest, hard-working, good hearted, man, assigned full responsibility before he was ready, carrying the burden.

As I remember, that was pretty much the end of our hour. Maybe acknowledging something of the genesis of his over-functioning will help him towards his goal of regaining his playful self of earlier days. Putting down some of the heavy burden surely will include recognizing the anger at having been so burdened.

Chapter 3

VICTOR

THIS IS A STORY about another one of my students; I enjoy him and working with him. In the early days of CPE, the Educators (*nee* Supervisors) were usually sort of renegades from regular, parish ministry who were enamored of more personal and in-depth explorations of the life and work of ministers; and Dr. Freud's perspective was in the ascendancy. Over time, as CPE became more respectable and mainstream, it became less acceptable for Supervisors—who were becoming thought of more as educators—to claim an expertise reserved to—and by—those specifically trained in psychology and psychiatry. As I noted earlier, however, in my story about Sam, there's a fine line between CPE's educational mission and psychotherapy. I think we do well to continue the in-depth exploration as essential to our mission as educators, and to our students' mission as pastors, the 'self' of the Pastor being the primary 'instrument' she uses in her work.

So Victor. He's in his forties, a Baptist, a native Russian who has lived in this country for over twenty years. He's married with three children. He's the Senior Pastor in a congregation in a mid-western state made up mostly of others of Russian origin. It is germane to this story to note that this is an unpaid position; he earns his living working in a school located in another nearby church of the same denomination.

People like Victor enroll in CPE in order to enhance their skills as pastors. I have students visit patients or parishioners—or whatever name fits the recipients of their pastoral/spiritual ministrations—and report on their visits via a verbatim account of the encounter. I also have them write me a weekly process note—sort of a free-floating, whatever-comes-to-mind kind of note. Not unlike, an observer might think, Freud's couch.

Those writings provide subject matter for our weekly individual conferences, though the student is free to bring other subjects, as I am also.

Victor has a physical handicap; his eyesight is quite limited, and he wears glasses with very thick lenses. In our prior week's meeting, I had asked him about his disability. He devoted this week's note to considering his thoughts and feelings about this condition.

As I have said in other tales of CPE, it always delights me when my student and I see and make the connection between his own personal life issues and the issues that invariably appear in the encounters he reports.

"I've been thinking about this all week", he said. "Could it be so unpleasant I simply don't want to talk about it? Maybe I've suppressed my true feelings . . . many might say so. But, after thinking it through, I've come to the conclusion that I simply don't think much about it; I simply accept it as an inevitable, incurable, unchangeable fact—just something to live with".

I was skeptical: "But, was there ever a time . . . ? " I asked.

"There were a few times when I was called names at elementary school because of my glasses . . . 'four-eyed' or 'frogman', and I felt very hurt. I came home and told my parents; I expected sympathy, maybe even some outrage. But they just laughed about it. I was stunned!"

"But then I thought, 'if they can laugh, so can I'. And you know what? My parents helped me to change my thinking about the whole issue; since then I just started to treat my disability as just something that is there".

I continued to press, and the closest he came to feeling was to acknowledge that it was "humbling" to have to ask for help—when he needed transportation, for example.

As we talked I commented on how his thinking is quick and facile; I suggested that his well-developed capacity to think, explain and understand kept him away from feeling. I even went so far as to suggest that his handicap was not his limited eyesight, but his well-anesthetized feeling self.

Then he surprised me with, "I used to get explosively angry; it was frightening to my wife and children. But, you know, you have to tame your feelings".

I am reminded once again—humbled, you might say—that none of us can ever know another very fully, that each of us is a rich complexity; and reminded that my intent is to remain open so to be surprised and delighted by such wealth—this quiet, reserved, thoughtful man sitting on a dormant(?) volcano.

By poking around, we unearthed a part of Victor that his calm, unruffled self had kept hidden—certainly from me and his peers, and perhaps, in a sense, from himself.

We didn't explore that anger further that day—at least, not directly.

We did move to review his verbatim—an encounter with Donald, a Baptist missionary, working in Israel, whom he had known in Seminary many years ago. Donald comes to the United States from time to time to visit supporting churches so as to raise money for his missionary work.

Victor describes Donald in terms that suggested—but did not say so directly—that he experienced Donald as an overly aggressive (perhaps, even, obnoxious) person, ending his description with " . . . a talker but has a tender spirit."

Of course, I jumped on that like a duck on a June bug— "talker . . . *but*".

"But what?" It took some digging on my part; then, "he's like a tank . . . "

"A tank; so?"

More digging; finally, "I am intimidated by him."

It seems that Donald has had a 'vision' which is telling him to do a particular project—by any reasonable estimate quite fantastic and unlikely of success. The more Donald insists that this is the course that he must take—he's had dreams telling him to pursue it— the more skeptical Victor becomes.

Victor reports that he decided that his pastoral role was to listen and to support, but he adds that he is not certain that is the proper role. Maybe he should try to prepare Donald for the real possibility of the failure of his quest. The intimidation Victor feels is evident.

When we talked about it, he was much more direct with me: "I don't buy the whole thing, the dreams and stuff . . . "; but he didn't share any of that with Donald.

I told him that it seems clear to me that Donald is Victor's volatile self. I appreciate his finding a way to bring both into our meeting today.

I didn't pursue any of this further that day. Victor is a very conscientious student, willing to learn and to grow, so I am confident that he is not—and we are not—at the end of this exploration. I am confident that he will expand his repertoire to include continued use of his very thoughtful self and renewed use of the emotional self he may be beginning to recover. Maybe he will find a way to let his own feelings about Donald and Donald's scheme guide him to a thoughtful—even gentle—expression of his feelings, and of his judgment.

Part 2: sure enough, he is still processing. He began today's meeting with a story about how a Russian colleague in Baptist ministry (someone he read about—he did not know the man personally), had suffered significant persecution from the Russian government. Ultimately the man was released and came to this country. But what aroused Victor's indignation was the way other Baptist leaders in Russia had turned on him. He said that the man had eventually poured out his heart about the pain he experienced at the hands of his "brothers".

Victor chose this way of telling of his own sense of betrayal by his colleagues at the school. He and the school board apparently became more and more at odds with one another, and he felt unsupported by them, despite his best efforts to support their directives. The situation became more and more stressful, resulting, he said, in the anger that he had mentioned earlier. That anger which he muted at the school found expression at home; it was that which led him to move to step down from Principal to the Assistant Principal position at the school which is his employer.

As I noted, he is also the unpaid Senior Pastor in a church of about 200 members. I'm still having trouble getting a clear picture of his place there. Senior pastor implies authority; several pastoral encounters he brought seem to me to reveal Victor as the trusted father figure. Though he had a tendency (which he modified over the unit) to offer a quick solution to the problems brought to him, the fact that they came to him suggests that he is seen as a trustworthy authority. And I mean to affirm that here: there is a way in which his calm self-presentation conveys a sense of trusted authority.

Which leads me back to the dichotomies. Victor seems to me to be a rich complex—both very bright and perceptive and, in some ways, also quite naïve and innocent. So he gets himself into situations wherein he gets conflicted and at odds with others—the school board, a split-off group in his Church, being two recent examples—things that hurt and anger him. And he doesn't indicate an understanding of— I might say that he doesn't see— how he gets into such situations, nor has he been able (willing?) to use his feelings constructively. But I am encouraged that this introverted person has tolerated my pressing him to know and express his feeling self more fully. And not just tolerated, but beginning to make constructive use of the emotional riches that reside in him. And over time he seemed to me to become more vocal and self-assertive in our group life.

Maybe it is time to take a brief excursion into theory. The parallel process as I've described it has to do with my student bringing a parishioner's struggle with some personal issue and our discovering, as we work with his work, that he, too, struggles with that issue. That, of course, is only one aspect parallel process. The other is no less delightful each time it appears, and that is when the relational dynamic that the student reports as between him and his parishioner is replicated in the way he is relating to me. More about that later.

Chapter 4

I Am J. Mary Jones!

SHE WAS A FEISTY little red-head, was J. Mary Jones. I hesitate even to use this description, lest I sound—even more than I may be—like a male chauvinist. But, to speak accurately, she was diminutive, with bright, curly red hair and, as I recall, she presented herself on first meeting with a certain emphasis and clipped precision: "Hello! I am J. Mary Jones!"

And she was young!

She was a student many years ago, so this tale will be even more fictional than most. Which is to say that memory being what it is, it surely is true for all of us that each of us recalls from our own frame of reference. As I recount this event, I supply missing details—which may capture something of the reality. I'll have more to say about fiction in the next chapter.

Aside: A therapist that Helen and I met with many years ago asked us something that triggered our recalling our honeymoon. What I remembered was markedly different from what Helen remembered. Our therapist commented that he had never met two people married to one another who had been on the same honeymoon.

So this is what I recall of J. Mary Jones—a lively and engaging young woman, who was at the same time very uncertain about herself and about what us CPE folks call "pastoral identity" and "pastoral authority". And, typical of many chaplain students—and perhaps of clergy, generally—she thought in terms of what she was supposed to do. What does the Chaplain *do* when she goes to the 6th floor East nurse's station? —a not unimportant question, just a limited one.

After she announces herself, "I am Chaplain J. Mary Jones", what comes next?

She managed to get to her Units. And she did indeed visit patients and have conversations with them. She wasn't always comfortable—no, that's not right—she was quite *un*comfortable with "god talk", but she was pretty sure that that's what Chaplains are supposed to do, so her visits were often brief and stilted, awkwardly concluding with a brief prayer.

I wasn't there, but I picture her even now as scurrying out of the room, trying to regain her composure.

Yet she was winsome and lively and engaging and irrepressible as a member of her peer group.

If I remember rightly, one playful day, in a sing-song voice, she gave a caricature of what the Chaplain visit consists of: "you walk into the room and say you're sorry for their pain and you say a prayer and you leave".

In an individual conference one day, after we'd worked together for a while, she brought her dilemma once again, "what am I supposed to *do?*"

It had to be a moment of inspiration; I had not planned this response. "Go", I said, "to the 6E nurses' station. And stand there. Don't *do* anything; *be* a blessing."

J. Mary said: "?"

But, gamely, she went to 6E and stood in the nurses' station.

I told this story recently in another context; the hearers said, "So what happened?"

They were disappointed when I had to say that the truth is I don't know what happened that day. I'm pretty sure a blinding and immediate revelation did *not* happen. What I remember is that over time, J. Mary Jones began to be comfortable with *being* a Chaplain and speaking with the authority of her being—even, sometimes, with a capital "A".

I tell this story, because I have never forgotten it. And, as with many things, the person who was most surprised by (and in need of) this reminder was I, myself. Somehow, I listened to myself as I offered her that simple advice; I had never been quite this clear about the simple matter of claiming *the authority of self.*

I read a story recently about a man recalling his experience as a young ballet student. His stern teacher would regularly howl at him, he said, during rehearsals, 'the audience won't look at you just because you do a perfect *grand jete'.* He said he didn't really get it until one day the teacher, a Frenchman shouted '*Mais nooo, je veux du vrai!*' ('No, I want something *real!*').

That renegade preacher, Will Campbell, used to say that the truly accurate translation of Second Corinthians 5:20 ("be reconciled . . .) is "be what you already are—one with god". Or, as the non-theistic religionists among us might say, be content to be one with all that is.

And in retrospect I can say that one of my life projects has been, and is, to live into my oneness with all being—and to live into and with the authority that accompanies that.

CPE students, not unlike everybody else, want to learn and will learn "how to do". And that's not unimportant. Maybe the other part is harder to grasp: how to be real.

Patients always know the difference between technical mastery and the real thing.

So, thank you. J. Mary Jones, wherever you are, for the gift you gave me that day. I'm still unwrapping and enjoying it.

Chapter 5

JUST MAKE IT UP . . .

"SOME TIME DURING THIS Unit", I usually tell my students, "if you want to, you can just make up a conversation between you and an imaginary patient. Don't tell us ahead of time if you do that".

In CPE the major tool we use is the verbatim. It is meant to be a transcription of a literal conversation between Patient and Chaplain. Some Educators have a very elaborate outline describing the way they want their students to present the verbatim material. I tend to be less elaborate in the instructions I offer, since I hope to allow the student to present in a way most authentic to her and her experience of the event being presented.

I ask the student to give us—me and his colleagues—a brief description of the situation in which the conversation takes place— setting, people involved, mood of the chaplain, of the ambience, and of the patient, as perceived by the chaplain.

Two analogies: the verbatim is like a play script, with both the words and the "stage directions"; or it may be compared to a sheet of music, with the words and the notes. I tell students that I want both the lyrics and the music.

I used to tell my students that they'd be surprised at how much they could remember, both words and music. I think I remember from my own student days occasionally being able to recall a long string of a conversation. But I'm less sure of that now. More recent studies seem to raise serious doubts about the reliability of memory, generally speaking; memory is now thought to be a creative process.

So it is probably true that making up a conversation comes closer to what really happens regularly.

And it may not really matter that the conversation fails the "literal" test, since what we want and can use is what, and who, the student is and brings to the encounter. I mean, it is the student whose work is being scrutinized. Lou, in Chapter 2, brought me a man feeling considerable guilt who was in need of forgiveness. How does Lou think and feel about guilt, sin, grace, and forgiveness? And how do those thoughts and feelings manifest in how he relates? When we bring those matters to the fore then we can discuss how Lou works with his parishioners. CPE sees the verbatim as a quite useful and generally reliable way to bring the issues alive in the moment.

An aside: this little excursion may belong elsewhere, but, as I think about students making up their verbatims, I begin to think of one of many manifestations of what I call the basic human heresy—namely the tendency to divide, to think in terms of this *or* that. In this case the tendency is to think in terms of fiction *or* non-fiction. (I say more about heresy in Chapter 13.) I am more and more convinced that is a false distinction; all fiction is about human life, imaginatively formed. In fact, the root of the word "fiction" comes from a word meaning "formed". At the same time, all non-fiction, if it is to convey any meaning at all, must depend on imagination to form the story into a coherent whole. Even if it comes from a reporter on the scene, the eye-witness and the imaginer cannot be separated; she has to form—*fictio*—her report about what she has witnessed.

In chapter 11 I mention several novels; I am confident that they present reality as accurately—or perhaps I mean even more usefully than any factual report can do.

CPE is interested in assisting the student to see how her own life story helps form her perception and thus her response to the patient. We want our students to be imaginative. We want them to be curious and attentive to the patient's story, and to be creative in forming the story they tell us about their encounter. I'm convinced that understanding the patient's story as a work of fiction helps the student more fully encounter both her patient and herself.

As I noted in the introduction, it's all about story

Chapter 6

THERE'S MORE TO IT

A ROMAN CATHOLIC PRIEST he is, from a developing country. Which means that in his home town, he is, by far, the most educated and therefore, in many ways, the superior, the leader, the authority—he is *Father* Carlos.

But he has been translated, so to speak; he now serves a parish in Texas, USA, where he is discovering that, though he is still Father, his parishioners are as well—if not better—educated, and that they exercise a certain independence. They will come into the church building and set up for communion, for example, without asking his advice or participation.

In the process note he sent me before our meeting, the ostensible theme is humility and Fr. Carlos' need to "stay humble": "I failed in this area of my ministry being humble," he said; "thinking that I know better than others, but I need to recognize more fully that in the United States people are more educated . . .".

I was intrigued, but not persuaded that humility was precisely the issue.

What I am continuing to learn again and again is the crucial importance of following the student's lead—or, as our mantra says, trusting the process.

So, mine is to not contradict his assertion that he needs to " . . . pray . . . that God might keep me humble . . . ", but to explore. What is behind or underneath this need to keep himself humble? Carlos is not wrong; it's just that there is more to it. There's always more to it.

Perhaps, as for many educated people, thinking about the problem is easier for Carlos than feeling the problem.

So Carlos thinks that though he appreciates his parishioners taking initiative, that often leaves him out; he is ignored. "They are not mindful of my presence".

I offer the word "ignored", and he agrees.

So Carlos is right—he is being humbled, not to say humiliated.

To go back a bit: in an earlier hour, Carlos had intimated that he is more than a little lonely in this very small Texas town. His skin color is different from many of his Parishioners; his accent is quite pronounced, and it is decidedly not Texan; they have a hard time understanding him. He is a stranger in their midst. He told me these facts —he gave me the words but the music was missing.

So I'm already sensitive to the reality of some unexpressed deep and likely painful feelings.

And today, he opens the door to explore them further. He doesn't immediately or easily "speak" feelings, but seems open to exploration. He is lonely; that hurts; truth be known, he also may feel some anger at being left out, ignored.

I don't recall whether he or I introduced the word "hurt" in response to the notion of his being ignored. But what emerged was his certainty that, if he were to acknowledge his pain and loneliness, even, perhaps, his anger, openly, he said, open expression would "disturb" the parish. So he must keep those things from them—keep them to himself.

We are both enculturated in the Christian tradition, so it seems quite right for us to appropriate some of the basic themes of that tradition.

Up to now, he has tended to speak more of and from the position of his role and persona as Priest; today we speak of his humanity, his need for human companionship.

Being a good Roman Catholic, he is, of course, imbued with a hierarchical view of the order of things. So God remains firmly in place—above; and rules are rules.

But, perhaps fortuitously, this meeting took place on Good Friday; right before us is the reality of the god/man who is "humbled even to death on the cross".

We delve right in to the dilemma of the god/man: how to be a hurting, angry, sad, hungry, warm, loving, mortal even—that is, a genuinely human person *AND* the Father, the authoritative Priest.

I guess real humility (from the word *humus*—earth) is called for. He may have to disturb his parishioners by being vulnerable as he acknowledges—exposes—his loneliness and his hurt and his anger—his earthy humanity; and he may have to suffer the consequence—they may get upset to see those things in him. He may have to suffer demotion from his exalted Priest station to simple equality with his parishioners in their common humanity; a genuine humbling.

Part 2, mid-April:

One of the many ways to speak of that indefinable— grace—is to note that it has to do with second chances. I mean, in this instance, to acknowledge that my students are always graceful with me, giving me many opportunities to get connected with them.

Which is to say that I was having trouble getting past the Father to the person.

So, in this week's conference, Carlos' process note is a report on two couples (all school teachers) who came to the USA from his home country to be teachers here. He only knew of it when a Priest friend from his home Diocese made him aware of their coming; since their arrival he has reached out to try to help them deal with their stranger status: "I have done my best to help them with questions about the culture here in the U.S."

We went over the story; I got some clarifications. It was well written; and I thought he was a good shepherd to the four. He told of the teachers' struggles—dismay even— with the unruly children; they were accustomed to very respectful and obedient pupils.

Carlos conveyed something of what these four people felt like. But the Priest in the story is just giving me the facts; I don't feel *him*. That is, once again, what strikes me about this report is the lack of the music. I can surmise that he gets some nurturance from sharing with fellow strangers in a strange land, but he doesn't say any of that. He is the impassive observer/reporter; the Priest above. I wanted to know from Carlos what he understood his interest to be in the story he reported. I wanted to get to the reporter behind the report. Maybe the reporter would allow himself some pride at having shepherded those teachers.

I reminded him of our earlier conversation and my sense of him as lonely; he revised and corrected me; I began to get a fuller sense of Carlos the man.

His parishioners like him, he said. Some are openly affectionate, as in, giving him hugs as they leave the Church after Mass. Part of the isolation he feels is simply the geographical location of the Church and Rectory: there aren't any neighbors passing by on a walk.

But he is reticent to reach out very far—to invite himself to dinner. He did say that he put a note in the Parish Bulletin when he first began there that he'd like to come to their houses to get to know them, but that seems not to have gotten much response. I had teased him a couple of weeks ago; a Parishioner had said he'd like to invite Carlos to dinner, but that his wife would have to do a thorough and extensive housecleaning before she would let the Priest in to her house. I told Carlos he should simply send word to her that he would be there at a particular time with his white gloves on to check above the door frames for dust.

Now the day before this individual session, Carlos had presented to his peers his pastoral visit by phone with a Parishioner: he answered the phone and she immediately began to cry; he let her cry without interruption. When she then told him that her son had been killed in a car accident, he was genuinely shocked and saddened, and did not hide that. All his responses were tender and caring—human. He let her rehearse the whole event at length. And in his reflection on the encounter, he says, " . . . I was emotionally dried and felt so sad . . . " and " . . . I felt powerless."

The Priest as fellow human was present with her in that encounter. He *was* her Priest, but not the father; rather he allowed himself to be emotionally "dried" (drained) from traveling this hard road with her.

It is clear to me that Carlos is taking seriously his need to get in touch with and to make use of his emotional self, as well as his formal, Priestly self. And he is beginning to do that. I am encouraged.

And a couple of further reflections on Carlos and me: maybe my own bias about Roman Catholic Priests hiding behind the rules had something to do with my difficulty knowing the man. Perhaps more importantly, the guarded Carlos—Fr. C.—who presented himself to me and his colleagues initially truly represents the way he initially presents to the world in general. And, as with us all, that's not all there is to Carlos. There's always more. *Deo gratias.*

One final gift I offered to him as our time together was ending: I told him that I'm not aware of much joy in him. Maybe, I said, that's the price of keeping a Priestly distance; I mean, I suspect the joy—even the playfulness—is there (I even see glimpses of it from time to time, and his colleagues report that when I am not around he is positively playful), but if the Father has to maintain a certain solemnity, he can't let that peek out very often.

As I discussed this impression with Carlos, he corrected me; he is, he assured me, a joyful and usually quite playful person; and he agreed that, in his culture (both ethnic and Roman Catholic), normally the student, in the face of authority, will be solemn and respectful. An added benefit is that in correcting me, Carlos also demonstrated a newly developing willingness (overcoming his former reluctance) to challenge the authority that I clearly represent to him.

Another theoretical excursion: CPE deals with what we call pastoral authority and pastoral identity—which I take to be two ways of naming essentially the same issue. J. Mary Jones, for example was clearly working on claiming her identity as a pastor and claiming the authority of that role.

Carlos was beginning to consider authority from another perspective as he began to risk calling me Peter and not "Father".

Chapter 7

Jacob and Esau

Barry is a winsome man, a Roman Catholic Priest of some twenty plus years as an ordained person. He is pleasant, easy going, rather quiet; there is an air of authority about him that he wears easily; colleagues seem to respond to him as if he is, in some way, their leader. His colleagues in his CPE cohort would affirm that characterization, I think, though he and they would also agree that he is somewhat guarded—hidden.

Today, the clinical material he brings me is a long telephone conversation with a woman he has known for about fifteen years—though he no longer serves in the Parish where she is a member. Marian often calls him, he says, and frequently her calls are for the purpose of complaining, usually about her family.

Specifically today her complaint is about her 30-year-old physician son who is planning to marry Alicia, something Barry knows Marian has wanted for some time. When she announces to Barry that they are engaged, he responds enthusiastically. He knew son John when he was a kid.

But Marian is not happy. Oh, she likes Alicia; and she also is pleased about their intention to marry. But she wants the marriage to take place in her home town church and not in the distant city where John is about to begin his practice. And, generally, she regularly complains to Barry that neither John—nor his brother, for that matter—have a commitment to the church. Her particular concern today is that John may not see all the church's paperwork through to completion; he may just find another venue for the marriage.

Of course Barry knew long before Marian gets around to asking that she wants him to either 'perform' the wedding in her home church, or, if not that, to contact the parish in John's city to ask them to see that John follows through with all the necessary preparations. At the very least, she wants Barry to urge John and Alicia to have a church wedding.

This is a dance very familiar to Barry:

'You're a good man, Barry; dance with me'.

'I don't want to, but I'll pretend . . . '

There may be two ways to think about this. He could see his dance partner as someone separate from himself—an other—the 'not me'. Marian is a separate being, one who is open with her anger and her complaints. He is the gentle one, always making peace and calming conflict—always finding a way to say 'yes'. They dance together, and he tries to lead her to a gentle pace. It doesn't work. The conversation ends; Barry knows that they never made contact—they did not dance together.

OR . . .

Maybe Marian is also, as Carl Jung might say, Barry's shadow side. Maybe she is not just an other, but his 'hidden side', the one who longs to say 'no', to confront, to oppose. The dance, then, might turn out to be acknowledging the oneness of good dancers—might allow the two 'sides' to embrace—one rambunctious and one smooth.

Sometimes, casting about for an image to help me capture something of the person of Barry, I have thought of the Biblical character, Jacob, described as a smooth man. And now, as I recall that image, I must also recall the 'hairy" man, his twin brother, Esau. Jacob is second born, following his brother out of the womb, holding on to Esau's heel. They are bound together—twins, friends, enemies—bound together, one. Years later, you may remember, Jacob learns to wrestle; the story intimates that his wrestling opponent is God. Jacob doesn't escape unscathed, but he gains integrity—which, as the dictionary says, is the state of being undivided.

Barry's bringing Marian today follows his having gradually, over several weeks, hinted at his sense of being a captive in the Roman Catholic system. A careful observer might have noticed several weeks ago a subtle movement—perhaps before Barry, himself, is quite ready fully to claim it—toward escaping the prison, toward wrestling with the church and claiming his freedom and independence—something of what Carl Jung means by individuation.

By bringing Marian, he brings the opportunity to practice his capacity for 'no'—the opportunity to embrace her, his shadow.

It seems a hopeful development; little by little he is bringing the more cantankerous, oppositional one from the shadows and onto center stage where s/he might become 'civilized' and positively useful.

One concluding thought about Barry, hinted at above: he replicates his style in the world in his working relationship with me; namely, he is smooth and charming. I find it easy to like him and enjoy him and to avoid any sharp confrontation with him. I wonder now if I might have been more useful to him if I had named—thus challenging—the avoidance function of his smooth charm. Can you say, 'parallel process'?

Chapter 8

PETER

I WAS BORN IN the mid-nineteen-thirties into a middle class, 'upwardly mobile' family in Chattanooga, a mid-size southern city at the edge of Appalachia. I might have been the baby child of three, except that, when I was about three and a half, my older brother, Billy, age six, never woke up from the simple procedure of having his tonsils removed. That left me and my fourteen months older sister, Janet, to make up the family, for a while; then came Stephen—Billy's replacement? — and then Timothy.

I had a 'normal' childhood in this post-depression, second world war era. I would describe it as happy, or, probably more accurately, as untroubled. I was a good boy in a family that expected that. Mine was a 'privileged' life, including a private high school and then Harvard. My family belonged to the large downtown Episcopal Church where I was active—as an acolyte and in the youth group.

The rector in the Parish in my high school years was a pied piper who became a Bishop while I was in college. Not having any clear idea of what direction my life should take, and being powerfully drawn by this charming piper, when said piper asked me, over lunch during Christmas break, which Seminary I was going to attend, I put up only token resistance—it seemed like a good idea at the time.

A hindsight comment: only in retrospect does my attempt to get a "Rockefeller Scholarship"—designed to give a person a year to explore ordained ministry without committing to it—signal a resistance unattended to at the time. Who knows what course my life would have taken had I traveled that road? From this perspective, it seems to me that my ten years in Parish Ministry was a detour on the road to "CPE land", where I have lived, happily, for the last fifty plus years. Yet it was not a detour without significant value—education gained through life experiences; at least partly I learned something about what I didn't know.

CPE, as earlier chapters have described, is the practical part of the education of people who want to be ministers, with the focus on enhancing pastoral skills.

The Seminary I attended expected but did not require that students participate in a summer Unit of CPE. Somehow, instead, I spent each summer in mission work—one summer in Bluefield, Nicaragua, and the next in very northern Alaska; so I did not take CPE.

Back home, ordained as a Deacon I was assigned to a large Parish in Knoxville to spend a year getting some of the 'green' off, before I was ordained Priest and given my own independent assignment. I cannot believe now how green I really was and how unprepared for much of anything worthwhile. At the time, of course, I worked very hard to understand and believe that my work was sacred—God's own.

So to a small Parish north of Memphis.

My Bishop and his family still drew me and charmed me; and eldest daughter, Helen, a beautiful young woman, became my wife while I was in that assignment.

The expected progression was from a small rural assignment to a more substantial suburban one and then, all things being equal, to a yet more substantial parish, thence to a high-steeple and perhaps, in time, one might be elected a Bishop.

It would be easy to blame my seminary and the norms of the church for my growing despair (which despair I would have denied, of course), but the truth is that it was my own lack of imagination which kept me from exploring any but the most traditional and narrow roles and functions of an Episcopal Priest. Being well-liked by Parishioners and the young people of the Diocese helped me to avoid acknowledging my growing sense of empty purposelessness. I possessed more of the smooth charm that I mentioned in my description of Barry than I knew, or claimed, and it served to keep me rolling along for quite a while.

By chance—if there is any such thing—I joined a clergy support group led by a Pastoral Counselor and a CPE Supervisor, both of whom worked at Vanderbilt University Hospital, the first as head of the Chaplains Service there and the second as Director of CPE. One thing that impressed me as I was in that milieu was the maturity, the sense of substance and authority, that I saw in the CPE Chaplain Residents. I wanted some of that!

Again, by chance, the other option that was appealing to me as a way to escape my ennui was the possibility of becoming the Episcopal Chaplain to Vanderbilt students—that other option was offered to the other candidate. So, after licking my wounds for a short while, I accepted the offer to become a Chaplain Intern at Vanderbilt.

I think I knew almost immediately that I had found home. But, of course, being cautious, I did not want claim and thus to commit to such an uncertain course.

But, uprooting Helen and two little children, to spend a year as an Intern and then another year, in another CPE Center—this time the massively large Central State Mental Hospital in Georgia—and then with no certainty of employment as a CPE Supervisor, somewhere—that was a matter of putting one foot in front of the other, with Helen gamely going along. Of course, when I began at Vanderbilt, I had no idea that this would lead to my life's work as a Chaplain and Supervisor. In fact, I didn't say out loud to anyone—myself included—that I wanted to seek the exalted position of Certified Supervisor, ACPE! until I was part way through that second year. That would be claiming too much authority—too much certainty about my identity! (I probably don't need to add that I continue to discover that claiming authority/identity is a life-long process.)

One more piece of luck: there aren't many Episcopal Clergy who are CPE Supervisors, and there aren't many positions designated specifically for an Episcopal Chaplain Supervisor. My year in Georgia was coming to an end, with no possibility—as I had earlier fondly hoped—of staying on there; and no job openings that I knew of. Panic was beginning to form in me, when the position of Episcopal Chaplain and Supervisor at Duke University Medical Center opened up. I was set!

I was still in the process, but I was granted full certification as a Supervisor shortly after I began at Duke, and I have spent the rest of my life working into being what I was authorized to be then—more about that in the next Chapter.

Chapter 9

ERNIE

NOT ABOUT A STUDENT this time—well, that's not so; the student in this case is me, a very slow learner, if that is not already apparent.

A neighbor whom I don't know very well stopped me the other day and said he wanted to talk to me when I had time. We see each other regularly, but usually just in passing. I like him well enough; he can be really entertaining some times, but I can't say that we have a close or deep friendship.

This afternoon Ernie and I chanced to have time to sit down to talk.

"I didn't know you were a minister until the other day when I saw you go by in your clergy clothes."

So, we began what is usually called, and may seem to be, small talk; he and Anne are Baptist. He knows little about Episcopalians; the very small crossroads town he grew up in had a Baptist Church on one corner and a Methodist Church opposite, and that's all he knew as a child. "Well, my Granddaddy was a Baptist minister", I told him; "but I grew up Episcopalian". Not much more to that string, I thought, so then it turned a bit more serious as he talked about Anne's many ailments.

Then he asked if I was conducting a neighborhood Bible study; he had heard somewhere that I was.

We talked a little bit about a men's Bible study group that he attended regularly for a while, but hasn't been lately; he is making it clear, but not quite directly, that he is lonely, that he worries about Anne and that he wants to have some deep conversation, "just you and me".

Maybe I need to give up being embarrassed at the fact that I'm slow and that it's almost always in hindsight that I recognize that it is more than small talk. As I walked away from that brief encounter, I recognized that this was the opening gambit, that he was testing the waters a bit—feeling me out, so to speak. "Of course," I thought to myself, acknowledging once again this new/old reality.

I've told my students, and myself, many, many times, that 'it's never about what it's about'; there's always more. Listen. The agenda will reveal itself in due time. If a student had brought this encounter to me, I might have suggested that the question about Bible study could have been an early clue that he wants more depth.

So in CPE, I, as the educator have the advantage of not being in the room with the student Chaplain and the patient; being one step removed, I can look for the clues and the hints in her report of the meeting as to the 'issue' for the Chaplain to address. That patient/Chaplain encounter is one step removed from the reality of immediacy.

Part two of the process is to encourage in the student the life-long practice of self-reflection—self-supervision.

And another equally important aspect of the encounter is the meeting between me and the student—the second part of the same learning event. It, too, is a live encounter between two people—one designated the teacher and one the pupil. The dynamics of the relationship between the student and his patient are being replicated in the relationship between me and my student. So—paying attention to what is being 'stirred up' in me as we meet can be an important clue about the relational dynamics between student and patient—parallel process.

Isn't that beautiful? It means I don't have to be in that patient's room to be in that room—in the immediacy of that reality. So, for example, remember Barry and Marian? In like manner, Barry and I replicate the dance of avoidance even while we are beginning to engage more deeply.

To take a brief excursion into theory here, the more technical term for what I've just described was coined by two clinical psychologists, Rudolf Ekstein and Robert S. Wallerstein. (One of my favorite students many years ago dubbed them "the Stein brothers'") They described the "clinical rhombus", a quadrilateral figure whose four sides are equal in length. For our purposes, the 'patient is one of the four points, the student Chaplain is another, the educator/supervisor is the third, and the administrator—representing the institutional milieu in which the program is housed—is the fourth.

As the student replicates the patient in her verbatim presentation of a particular encounter, so the relationship that develops between her and her supervisor re-presents, or re-creates, the relational dynamics she is reporting. The supervisor thus has the rich mine of both the reported patient/student dynamics and the more immediate student/supervisor dynamics being played out in the consultation; all this within the reality of all the administrative dynamics in the milieu where it all takes place.

As I think about that chance encounter with Ernie further, I also think that an important aspect which—again! —I see more clearly in hindsight is his opening gambit; his question about my being clergy. I don't know for sure, of course, but it seems reasonable to assume that he is seeking out someone with some authority—a minister.

My profession for the last forty plus years has been about enhancing the pastoral skills—I've always understood that to be equivalent to relational skills—of people who want to be ministers. Back when I started, it was mostly Protestant Christians; then there were some Jews and some Roman Catholics and more recently some Muslims, Buddhists, Humanists, and others.

One common and continuing issue is the matter of authority—the same as, or closely kin to, pastoral identity. You may recall that J. Mary Jones was dealing with claiming her own authority.

But authority is a complex matter. I assume that Ernie imputed to me some authority. Complex: there's Ernie; there's me; and there's our specific relationship and our relationship within the context of 'church'—the clinical rhombus. I was ordained a Priest at the age of 26; I was given a Bible as a "sign of the authority given" to me; and almost immediately, at the end of that ordination service, I stood up and blessed people—in the certainty that I was speaking for God. I was given authority long before I felt or claimed it or felt ready to exercise it. Ernie, however, accords to me, imputes to me, some authority; there's something about me that is special by virtue of the fact that I am a minister. Ernie is older than me, but, in some ways—probably ill-defined by either of us—he defers to me.

I recall my father's relationship to ministerial authority—or my perception of it: his father was a Baptist preacher, but for many of his years worked as the superintendent of the Hamilton County Home for Neglected and Dependent Children (Bonny Oaks). My father always called him "Father". I don't know much directly about the internal dynamics of that relationship. But I suspect, from my observation of my father with the clergy in his adult life (including me) that he had some ambivalence about us—a deference, almost as if he believed we had some magical power—mixed with a sort of subtle disrespect, as if he saw us as relatively incompetent about worldly matters.

I recall occasionally—and every time with bemusement—that when I (by then many years a Hospital Chaplain) came back to visit my mother who was in the hospital dying, my father beseeched me to go in to her room to pray for her. Even then that felt odd to me; I wanted to say, "I'm your son not your Priest . . . "

I don't know that I even appreciated for many years the irony of being Father to parishioners, most of whom were my elders, not alone in age, but also in worldly experience and wisdom; what chutzpa! I think one important aspect of my life's journey has been gradually growing into an acceptance—a claiming—of authority; allowing both Ernie and me to honor an authority that I somehow embody even if, in some important senses, it is mine only to carry and represent. Ultimately, perhaps, it allows us both to honor some sense that there is power/authority that resides at once within and beyond us, even if we do not name it 'god'.

It is an awesome thing to discover yourself to have the power to bless and/or to be a blessing.

And that's what CPE means to introduce our students to—the power and its awesomeness.

This authority business has occupied my attention, one way or another, for a good part of my life. Several years ago, I had thought about writing an essay titled, "Fr. Mulcahy and the Wizard of Oz" as a way to meditate on authority. For some who may not remember, Father Mulcahy was the Priest in the long running TV Series, M.A.S.H. Initially portrayed as a rather insignificant and ineffective member of the M.A.S.H (Mobile Army Surgical Hospital), unit in Korea, over time his character developed; he came to be seen as the soft-spoken, gentle source of comfort and strength. It is to the credit of those who created the show that they never tried to explain his character; they were content to 'let the mystery be'. I never wrote that essay (until now, of course) but, if I had, the other part would have considered another aspect of authority as exhibited by the Wizard of Oz. His authority was revealed to him—only when its trappings were stripped away—as it was simultaneously revealed to Dorothy and her friends: it resides, mysteriously—perhaps mystically—in his as in their humanity.

Chapter 10

"A Hot Mess"

A FEW YEARS AGO, I contracted to supervise a group of Students for one Unit. The first day I met with them and they were introducing themselves to me, one woman (I'll call her Sarah) led with her name and then, "I am a hot mess". It is not a common occurrence that so blatant an invitation to exploration is offered, but one aspect of being an effective pastor is to be alert to the reality that invitations, blatant or subtle, are always being offered.

So, if somebody were to say to me, "Peter, what do you tell your students as they start in their CPE process with you?", one of the first things would be the admonition to be curious. Earlier I mentioned the rich and complex nature of each human being and the delight in discovering the riches; so there's really a double message: the curiosity is driven by the conviction that there is richness to be discovered and enjoyed in each one.

Sarah certainly got my attention with that introduction. And she went on to indicate that by 'hot mess' she meant pretty volatile—another term for it is 'labile'—and not necessarily in a positive way. It was another one of those graceful moments, perhaps motivated by that very admonition about curiosity, that led me to tell her that I understood that to mean that she was a very rich person—a good way to introduce my curiosity and to allow exploration. Curiosity— "tell me more".

As I tell my students, "your patient will tell you everything you need to know".

Curiosity—tell me more—listening; certain that every one is a treasure of rich complexity.

Chapter 11

THE SHORTEST DISTANCE . . .

" . . . by indirection find direction . . . "
HAMLET

ANOTHER THING I OFFER my students is based on my belief that a straight line is *rarely* the best way to get from here to there.

Many of my colleagues include in their assignments a raft of instruction books—books about how to be a pastor, or how to make a good pastoral visit—things like that.

It is both a weakness and a strength in the way I work that I avoid those books almost entirely; I avoid the straight line! The goal of this educational process is best accomplished by indirection, aphorisms, pithy sayings, parables, stories. It's not that I don't teach: I treasure those teachable moments that come in the clinic, when the opportunity to learn is fresh and hot.

I trust that the students have already had the academics; they've been exposed to the textbooks, the theories. Now is the time to practice encountering real people in their real-life situations, and practice thinking about (reflecting on) real life experiences, both directly, through responses of peers, and via the reflections of others as found in novels and other imaginative writings.

"Trust the process", we say. By which we surely mean—among other things— trust the student; leave her alone to do her work' Well, yes! In addition to the healthy diet of actual human to human encounters for her to reflect on, give her the nudge of a good novel; she will have to be curious—what is here? What is this author telling me? Why did my teacher give me this?

For example:

Peter DeVries, in his tragi-comic novel *Blood of the Lamb*, offers some profound theological reflection on what theologians call "theodicy" in his story about the life of Don Wanderhope; I loved discovering that his name was fraught with meaning.

Michael Malone's hilarious novel, *Handling Sin*, exhibits and evokes the kind of theological reflection that every CPE student will be engaging in throughout.

Anthony DeMello's *One Minute Nonsense* has the kind of zen-like stories that invite theological/pastoral reflection. Also the companion, *More One Minute Nonsense*.

Irvin Yalom's *Love's Executioner* teaches by example the sensitive use of the self of the therapist in encountering other humans in their struggles.

In the Chapter about Jerry, I'll mention another seminal book which I often use to help expand students' world.

In a brief quotation from the book, *Genius*, about the quantum scientist Richard Feynman, the author says this: Feynman, in his Nobel Prize lecture, tried to convey " . . . the sense of science as a *process* [emphasis added] rather than a body of formal results. Real science was confusion and doubt, ambition and desire, a march through fog."

ACPE defines clinical pastoral education as process education, by which we mean to convey some sense of the messiness in the work and the confusion and doubt as to results. The genius of CPE has always been its willingness to engage the "living human document" with its wealth of contradictions and complexities—its messiness. By the very nature of our work, we must always live in and with messy uncertainty. That's our genius and our beauty.

And the books I mention here support the process of exploration and reflection while avoiding the academic (and, I might add, the Church's) temptation to establish certainty. In Chapter 28, I quote another book at some length, to make the point that any one theory about human beings is necessarily limited; I include a brief excerpt here: "Human beings are so complex, *any* theory fits. By fitting, the theory excludes the complexity, *so you lose what's human.*" [my emphasis here]. Connecting human to human—as complex a process as there can be—is what CPE is about.

Chapter 12

"THIS IS YOU AND THIS IS ME"

I'VE BEEN BLESSED WITH good supervisors and colleagues in the CPE world over the years, and, of course, there are stories to go with each. "Supervisor" is the nomenclature the ACPE used for years; but recently the title changed; we are now "Certified Educators".

Here is what is perhaps a side note: a respected colleague, reading some of this material, wondered if I had some reaction to the fact that the ACPE had recently changed our official designation from "Supervisor" to "Educator". Usually I'm intrigued with words and the nuances inherent in them, so I'm surprised by the question and surprised that I had not considered it before. So, herewith: super-visor=over-seer=*episcopos*=bishop. Authority is implied. Educator is one who 'leads out'—*duco*=leads; *ex*=ed=out. Etymologically, educator has to do with training horses. So both designations have value in describing something of the meaning of what we do, with supervisor, perhaps, emphasizing the importance of authority and educator emphasizing the skills involved in leading students.

Kempton Haynes was the "Director of CPE" at Vanderbilt University Hospital; he was my first Supervisor way back in 1971. He was my age, or maybe even a bit younger, but he exhibited a sort of *gravitas*—a sense of confident authority—that convinced me he was a trustworthy father figure. He didn't theorize about authority; he didn't have to for his students to learn something about authority and about the power to bless (he did introduce us to Myron Madden's little book, *The Power to Bless*). Kempton also introduced us to the psychosocial developmental theory of Erik Erikson. It was a handy scheme for beginning to understand something about the general field of psychology that has always intrigued me. Over the years, I have encountered other approaches (e.g., Myers Briggs; Enneagram; Family Systems; Yalom on group psychotherapy; Bowlby, attachment theory; more recently cognitive behavioral therapy and its many variants) but I had to begin somewhere. I'm meaning to say here that each scheme is valuable and each scheme is limited; all enrich our understanding; none is complete. Further, over the years, surely each practitioner develops his own unique style, incorporating bits and pieces of various theories—hopefully a style which honors the complexity of each other person by not imposing any rigid theoretical frame. In a later chapter (29) I will speak more fully about problems inherent in depending on any one theoretical frame.

Jim Hardie was a gentle, soft-spoken Chaplain at Central State Hospital in Milledegeville, who worked with some of the most "regressed" patients there. I've never forgotten his story having to do with boundaries: he took the hand of one such patient in his own hand; gently then, he touched the man's arm and then, in turn his own; he did this several times, repeating each time, "this is you, and this is me; this is you and this is me"—a powerful and immediate way to make Murray Bowen's differentiation/self-individuation real and useful. I have used that story many a year as I orient new students to the importance *both* of *connecting* and of maintaining a *clear, separate identity*.

Wes Aitken was the head of Duke University Medical Center's Pastoral Care Department for many years. From this distant retrospect, it occurs to me that he may have been something like Father Mulcahey; he was humble and low key, but a presence, known and respected throughout the large Medical Center. He was ordained a Methodist Minister, but he was clearly Father Wes. A colleague, Ted, and I were still in process toward full certification, so we needed to meet regularly with Wes. He was beginning to be known, affectionately, as Rip Van Wes, because he tended to drop off to sleep during the supervisory hour. He laughed with us when we teased him about it. Finally Ted and I got Wes to agree to meet with us together so we would have somebody to talk to in that hour!

Another member of that Department in those days, John, was his own independent self, somewhat curmudgeonly sometimes—strong on the differentiated self aspect. The gift he gave me was his brief description of his work as a Pastoral Counselor, something like, "I just meet with people and mess around in their lives . . . ".

I remember, also, being tickled then and still by what he says he often told his clients and students, "Don't get mad at me; I'm not trying to help you." This may not actually be a rule of thumb, but I think students would do well to reflect on their meaning when they find themselves wanting to 'help' their patients; that impulse could contain a condescension that works against getting along side.

Over the years I am becoming more comfortable about knowing how little I know. A little curiosity, a trust of the process, a growing awareness of the rich complexity of each person, and a willingness to mess around without the 'comfort' of certainty pretty well describes the way I mean to work.

I repeat my sense of being blessed with so many rich colleagues. If my memory worked better I might call more of them to mind now, but there are two more who have been particularly wonderful companions.

I was a member of the committee, many years ago, that voted to certify Miriam as a Supervisor. My memory is that in that very meeting, I recognized a star (though I think she has a different take on that day). She has been a steadfast friend all these years—a solid, no-nonsense, wise, caring pastor and Supervisor, and a warm and caring friend with a wonderful sense of humor and a sort of wise and worldly wisdom. After I formally retired from UT Medical Center, I was offered the opportunity to supervise, long-distance, a group of Salvation Army Officers (Ministers). We met in person occasionally at the Atlanta headquarters of the Salvation Army, and I visited each student at their service site from time to time during their two-year, four Unit CPE Program; but mostly we met via long-distance phone calls (this was before Zoom or the like was invented)! It was grueling.

The Atlanta meetings were stressful for me in a particular way; with this fairly constrained cohort of Officers, I felt, rightly or wrongly, some constraint on my freedom of verbal expression. I wouldn't say that I'm inordinately profane, but I was pretty sure that, at least initially, as we were getting acquainted, it was not time for the kind of language that is not unknown to me—language that is sometimes characterized as "salty". So it was beyond mildly relieving when Miriam and her wonderful partner would meet me for dinner there in Atlanta—a martini, and her warm humor and complete understanding acceptance was exactly the kind of embrace I needed.

My first encounter with the irrepressible Bill Russell was in a Committee meeting when I was seeking Certification (as an "Associate Supervisor"—step one of the two step process). I have always considered myself fortunate that from that beginning—me as supplicant, he already a very accomplished Supervisor—we became very good friends and colleagues (often sharing a room together at our Annual Meetings). He is one of the most imaginative people I know, a person who is humble and yet trusting of his instincts— instincts that would lead him to spontaneous moments of deep connection with students. A man with a wonderful sense of humor, deep compassion, and that wonderful impulsiveness that may have surprised him sometimes as much as it did others.

Chapter 13

HERESY (AND A FAILURE)

WHAT, YOU MIGHT ASK, is this topic doing in a book about CPE and my work as a Supervisor/Educator?

Heresy—as that word is used colloquially—is, ironically enough, the basic human heresy. The word "heresy" comes from the Greek word which originally meant something akin to "choose"; but it has come to mean wrong thinking—initially, almost always in terms of theological error; now, more generally, it refers to any position not in accord with any orthodox—that is, *'straight opinion'* (more Greek). It has come to mean choosing this and eschewing that.

Earlier I talked about Jim Hardie and his careful distinction between him self and the patient. So I could be understood—rightly—to be asserting the importance of distinctions—of choosing—of acknowledging that there is this and there is that, there is you and there is me, separate and distinct.

But the other part of my assertion is that though this and that are distinct, they are not separate; and that they are not whole—they are not well—until they are joined. Remember that Jim was holding the patient's hand the whole time: 'you are different from me and me from you, but wholeness comes when we are together'.

So, as educator, I mean to model for my students. I am curious as I meet a student: 'tell me your story; I want to know about your unique self'.

Sometimes it is easy and sometimes not to appreciate the 'other-ness' of the other; 'how delightful; what an interesting—even rich—way to be'; or 'that's weird; how did you get to be *that* way?' I often have to remind myself that richness is always there. And my work always is to find and appreciate and affirm that richness (intending, of course, to model that openness to the other's richness).

And, of course, I often fail. I started to say "sometimes", but, more accurately, it is often; frequently the student and I are able to recover during the course of the Unit from the failure to connect—failure being at least as much a part of experiential learning as 'success'.

But sometimes the failure doesn't get repaired. I had a student about five years ago; I'll call her Tina. The group Tina was in had been together prior to my working with them. It was clear to me very early in my relationship with that group that Tina was designated as the "troubled child" in the "family system".

The other part of the general principle that we tend to assign roles to one another is that that assignment requires the assignee to accept the designation—to play the assigned role. So Tina played the role. A group is likely to seek a scapegoat; and, complementarily, a member is likely to volunteer to take that role.

Now, five years later, I'm wondering how much I let myself be biased by their perception. But, whatever the cause, I failed to find a way to appreciate the richness of her difference. Was it that she is a black woman? Or from a small, somewhat exclusive denomination? Or her secretiveness? Her aloofness from the group? I still regret that I never found the way to hold her hand while affirming her uniqueness. If there is any 'redemption', it is that I am still thinking about and learning from that time with her, and I can only hope that she, too, might still be puzzling about how that Unit might have been profitable for her. As I think about it, I wish I had been less confrontive, more willing to let her be. I wonder now if I should simply have acknowledged to her that I could not find a way to connect and that I would just stand beside her. *Primum non nocere*—first do no harm—should have been my guide, I think. My need to 'do something' (shades of J. Mary Jones)—in order to be a good educator—was likely my downfall.

But to get back to where this chapter started: it seems to me that science and religion are gradually coming toward the same conclusion, namely that there is a mysterious unity of everything—a oneness; that finally there is not a this *or* that, but a this *and* that; not a light *or* dark, but a light *and* dark; not up *or* down, but up *and* down; not good *or* bad, but good *and* bad; not right *or* wrong, but right *and* wrong.[1] Each of us encompasses, embodies, a uniting of all those apparent opposites, so that what seemed to be separate and opposed, can only finally come to be seen/known as one. (See Chapter 23, below, on theological reflection where I again address the unity of all.)

My student and I are about the business of replicating this dichotomous unity: it may begin as my student *or* me, but the aim is finally to give up our heresy, our choosing, and embrace it all—he and I; he and that other, 'peculiar' colleague; he and that very different patient.

---

1. There is a wonderful story about Rabbi Moishe: he and his wife are sitting in their parlor one evening when Yitzak comes in to complain about Jacob. Yitzak lays out his case with considerable passion. When he has finished, Rabbi Moishe says, "Yitzak, you are right". It is not much later that same evening when Jacob appears. If anything, he is even more eloquent and passionate than Yitzak. When he is done rehearsing his complaint, the Rabbi says, "Jacob, you are right". Jacob departs and Moishe's wife says, "Moishe! They can't *both* be right!. If one wins the other loses!" The Rabbi says, "My beloved, you are right".

Chapter 14

ANOTHER REGRET

MARY ANN WAS A pretty young woman seminarian, participating in a summer Unit of CPE with me as the educator. This was some years ago, so my memory is hazy, but I think I can capture something of what I mean to present here.

She was pleasant, as I remember, and somewhat reticent or reserved—she seemed to hold back. The Unit did not get off to a very good start for her. In that first week, she told me her favorite uncle was quite ill; I think she said she needed to go see him at their home which was a couple of hours away; in the next week (or maybe it was two), the uncle died and she was away at the funeral, missing two or three days of the Unit, including several group sessions.

I do not do well with disruptions of the schedule. Am I too rigid? Perhaps. My rationale is that an eleven-week Unit is a very limited amount of time in which the students have to develop a working alliance with me, each other and the hospital Units they are serving. There's lots to learn, and the learning is dependent, in great part, on establishing those trusting relationships.

She returned from the funeral. She met with me for her next scheduled individual conference with little material to present. She made it clear that she did not want to talk about her uncle or her grief.

What to do?

I let my anxiety—limited time available, lots to accomplish—get the best of me.

"So", I offered, "you had mentioned that you were something of an 'ugly duckling' in high school, but you seem now to me to be a very pretty young woman; might you want to talk about that transformation?" In other circumstances, a perfectly legitimate invitation to self-reflection.

A chilly silence . . .

I could have responded to the silence by modeling some good self-reflective behavior along the lines of, 'I apologize; I realize that I was acting as if there is more trust established between us than is there, and I let my anxiety to make every minute count, etc., etc.'

She let me know the next week that she felt quite assaulted.

And later that she never felt I apologized fully.

We muddled through the Unit, but never really established a working alliance.

Chapter 15

STEVE

STEVE SWEARS THAT THIS happened: I have only the vaguest memory of it.

Steve is one of my favorite people. He was one of the best students I ever was graced to work with. Now he is a valued colleague. I have his permission to tell this story.

Early in my time as the Director of CPE at University of Tennessee Medical Center in Knoxville, a young man applied to be a year-long Chaplain Resident. I'm sure there were stumbles in his first year with us, but they have long faded from memory. He was an excellent student and quickly became an accomplished Chaplain. The impressions I have from here is of a young man who rapidly developed a confident presence. I do recall that staff members confirmed that impression.

He did so well and liked the work so well, that he applied for a second year in our program, and we happily and immediately accepted him.

Here's how he recalls the event: at some point in that second year he came to my office one day for his weekly consultation. As always, I expected him to present me a process note. On this day, he came empty-handed.

When I inquired, he said he had nothing. Further inquiry elicited his fatigue with the program—he had gotten all he could; he was "done".

Our office suite consisted of a center office for the Administrative Assistant, with my office off to one side, and the office of George, the Director of the Department, off to the other.

What Steve remembers is that I got up from my desk and, with him in tow, went across to George's office; I told George that Steve said he was finished; George pulled out a resignation form and handed it to Steve.

Steve says that he was back in my office in 45 minutes with the required process note.

Of course, I'd like to take credit for a brilliant supervisory move, and I do—even if, as with so many of my maneuvers, such moves often come to me as inspiration and surprise. But, beyond that, this story illustrates CPE as experiential education in every aspect. Steve was a good student, which means, in part, that he was willing to assert his own personhood and authority and to test the limits—all things we want our students to learn; and he was smart enough to assess this moment and to learn by direct, immediate experience that *CPE* is adult education—in this case that adults have to live with the consequences—and that *CPE* uses all moments as teachable moments.

Steve stayed on after that second year as a staff Chaplain. He is now George's successor, the head of the Department. As you might well surmise, he treats the current student Chaplains as adult learners.

Chapter 16

When, What, How
and How Much?

I'VE ACKNOWLEDGED EARLIER IN these pages that our work has many aspects that make it similar to that of therapists and counselors. One significant issue we share with them has to do with confidentiality, and, more specifically, with how much to share with the client or student. My favorite brother-in-law, Allston, is an attorney and a thoughtful person. It occurs to me that this is an issue of interest to attorneys, too. I invited him to help me consider the question. I wrote him the following:

"Allston,

"In your practice, do you keep "private" notes on your conversation with a client; if so, might that client have a 'right' to see those notes?

"As a Clinical Pastoral Education Educator (*nee* Supervisor) I often made notes about students; those notes are described in ACPE's formal documents as the private property of the Educator and not 'discoverable'.

"One of my heroes is Irvin Yalom, a psychotherapist and a novelist who has written extensively and quite personally about his work with his clients. One book, *Every Day Get a Little Closer*, contains his work with a patient/client in which he and the client agreed to share, as part of the therapy, weekly notes and impressions about that relationship and their work together.

"So, as to my first question to you, are there circumstances in which you would share your 'private' notes with a client? Let's say that you have a 'private' (or personal) assessment of the mental condition of your client. Whether in a written note or not, under what circumstances would you find it beneficial to the client and/or your work with him to share that assessment? Conversely, when might you determine to withhold?

"Yalom seems to me to tend to be quite open with his clients. I'm fairly sure that he would be selective in what and when he shared his perspective; and from what he tells us (in *Love's Executioner*, for example) about how and what he shares, it seems always to be with the intent of his sharing his own human struggles and foibles in order to establish rapport.

"In the most recent CPE Unit I did I was inspired to write some short stories—*a la* Yalom—about a particular session with each of several students. ACPE standards require the Supervisor to write a "Final Evaluation" of the student at the end of each "Unit". I have always kept 'private' notes to help me in that effort; but this time I used the stories almost whole cloth as the bulk of what I wrote."

It is these stories that I'm including in this book.

"Might you comment", I asked Allston, "on these thoughts/questions?"

Allston wrote back. His comments were brief, and included some references to Rules of Professional Practice for Attorneys.

I replied: "When I have a 'difficult student'—set aside for now the genesis and responsibility for the difficulty— I may well record my impressions and/or my 'diagnosis', so to speak, in my notes.

"Aside from the question of whether they are discoverable, which I guess *is* a matter of law, my real interest has to do with how I or you go about deciding whether to offer that set of impressions and that 'diagnosis'; if yes, then the equally important question is how to offer it.

"I do have a 'learning contract' with my student; she expects to hear my critique. I believe that, in the same way, you have a contract with your client; he expects to hear your best judgment about his situation. As you say, you tend to be very direct and often will 'warn' your client that that is how you treat all your clients.

"So, with students and clients, the 'whether' question is answered—we are obligated to offer, within our areas of expertise, what we have.

"That does not relieve us from determining the best way to offer what we have. Some aspects for you may be simply matters of established law, but, even then, how to couch your advice based on the law still requires thought on your part as to how best to convey your opinion and advice. And that is not so easily determined.

"Even the best advice from you or the best assessment from me—in my case, probably a good bit more subjective—is not useful or helpful if the client/student cannot accept it. In your situation, even if the law is cut and dried, I assume that you still give some thought as to how best to give your assessment and advice. A is tough and expects—and can take—a hard, tough bit of advice. B is emotionally a bit fragile, as best you can determine; you have the same advice to offer, but you may well find a gentler way to say it, because you do want him to hear and heed it."

In Chapter 13 I mentioned my poor work with Tina in a Unit a few years ago; the failure was in my timing and in the poor way I offered my assessment to her. I noted there some of the ways I might have better worked with her. And, with Mary Ann (Chapter 14), once again, I illustrate poor use of potentially very helpful information.

But my point here, of course, is simply to note the basic questions every educator must regularly confront, both in order first to make significant contact with his student and second to model the importance of attention to those questions to his student as he (the student) encounters his patients—parallel process once again.

Sometimes, in my 'failures', the best I can hope for is that my student will learn what *not* to do!

Chapter 17

A Partial Verbatim

A1: PETER, I NEED to talk with you sometime about cremation. I'm confused about it.

Anne is a neighbor, married to Ernie (see Chapter 9). She is 91 and he is 92; they've been married for almost 60 years. In my brief chance encounter with her the other day, she made that request.

So this morning I called to see if it might be convenient for me to make a visit. It was, so I went to their apartment. This conversation lasted about 40 minutes.

I like these folks. He is quite outgoing; she is quieter and quite frail in appearance, but a lot more 'spunky' than she appears.

I've talked with them enough to know that they are—or at least she is—very connected to her religious tradition and practices. Church life is very central in her life. I'm pretty sure that this includes looking to the minister for guidance. On my way to their apartment, I cautioned myself not to give in to the temptation to give her 'answers'.

E1: Does this conversation need to be private?

A2: This is about you, too; you are the problem. (with a twinkle).

He went to get his hearing aids. I pulled a chair close to her.

A3: Before we begin, I want to tell you that we started two churches in our hometown. We moved in to a new neighborhood; our house was one block from the school and one block from the library. There was a new little church nearby with just a few members and we helped build it up until it became the biggest church in town. Then the minister—we just loved him—took a call to a small church nearby; there were only 32 members at first. We followed him there and helped do everything. We even cleaned toilets . . . How long were we there, Ernie?

E2: About 40 years.

A3: Church is so important; it is so great to get together and do things for the Lord.

P1: Do you miss it?

A4: Oh, so much. (A mix of obvious deep happiness and sadness as she recalls their life there.) After we got so that we could not get there any more, a couple of ladies came once a week to bring us lunch. We loved that Church and those people. Both our children live here and they decided we needed to move here. Our son signed us up for this place without even asking us about it. (I didn't sense any anger here; she seemed content and accepting of their need for close attention.)

P2: So, what's on your mind about this cremation business?

A5: I'm just confused. He's made up his mind; he's going to be cremated. But the Bible says that he's coming from the east and that we are going to rise up and meet him. We are supposed to be buried facing east. I mean I know we are going to go up there immediately and be with him. But, if we don't have a body . . . I mean I just don't know what to think.

E3: It doesn't make any difference; once you're dead there's nothing left there; your spirit just goes from your body. (Is he a little exasperated?)

A6: He's going to die before I do, and I'll be buried in my casket with his ashes at my feet; so that, if he misbehaves, I can kick him!

(There's a good bit more conversation here about the Bible and what it says about rising up to meet the Lord in the air. I'm generally embarrassed about my lack of Biblical literacy; I can't engage much about Biblical content.)

P3: I like to joke that Episcopalians don't know much about the Bible, so I don't really know what to say here. But I'm not clear what you are concerned about.

(thinking that one obvious issue not yet directly addressed is death—no sense of denial here; we just haven't named it directly.)

You almost died earlier this year, didn't you? (So I risk going at it directly.)

A7: Oh yes. I was in the hospital two times.

P4: But you seem much healthier now?

A8: Yes, I'm much better now. Of course, I know I could go any time.

(I don't get the sense from either of them that they fear death—though in an earlier conversation with Ernie, back when she was in pretty bad shape, it was clear that the thought of her dying was very distressing to him).

The conversation continued for a little after this; there wasn't any grand decision reached.

I was satisfied that we had made contact and that we had acknowledged the reality of death; my sense was that making a decision was not the point of the visit; continuing the conversation was, and we did that—a low-key visit, but not insignificant.

I haven't actually written a verbatim in many, many years. This is fairly faithful to the conversation, and one thing about it that strikes me immediately is that it would be easy to miss the significance. It is like many verbatims students have presented to me over the years.

And, honestly, I'm a little hesitant to include this in my book.

So one perennial question: "Why did you bring this verbatim?"

My purpose in this context is to give a simple sample—to illustrate the use of this most basic of our tools; and if I were bringing it for my

Educator's critique, I'd likely say, as students often said to me, "Because I had to have a verbatim."

So for illustrative purposes, I'll continue with how the supervisory consultation might go.

"Well, is there anything here to work with?" (the Educator always assumes that there is). He might say, 'why not let them educate you about how they read and interpret the Bible? You let your own embarrassment short circuit a possibly fruitful conversation.'

In hindsight, I agree. Further, he might say, 'you risked bringing death to the table; you might have explored their thoughts and feelings more.' I would probably have agreed that it was a risk, and added that I felt I knew them well enough to have a sense of their wisdom and resilience, and that the risk was worth taking. 'Clearly you like these people; you might want to pay attention to what you like about them; and you might want to wonder how your fondness helped you connect to them and also whether it might have hindered the exploration of issues that may have needed to be addressed.'

If the student is something of a veteran of the action-reflection process, he might very well have included these comments as self-reflections in this evaluation section

I am not as insistent these days on a specific theological comment, though such a thing is a fairly normal component of the evaluation section of the verbatim presentation. A comment also on what is called these days 'social location' is usually included, either in the introductory material or in this section.

Chapter 18

The Admission Interview, or, the Absconding Educator

Do I really want to tell this story? Well, if I'm to tell a true story I have to. This happened a long, long time ago. The details may be hazy now, but the essence remains.

She had sent us her written material, as we require; she was applying for our Resident year program. We liked what we saw there, so we invited her to come interview in person. Sometimes we will conduct the interview with a group—perhaps a staff Chaplain, a Nurse, a current Resident, and me; in addition, as the Director of the program, I may schedule a one-on-one interview. That's what I'm recounting here.

I'll call her Annette; she was young, bright, attractive, African American.

As I say, the details escape me, but typically as the interview began, I would have asked about her family of origin and her place in it. As I usually tell my students, there are a wide variety of ways to think about folks and their story and each scheme has its strengths and each its limitations. Some might use a Myers-Briggs kind of approach or an Enneagram. I probably began with Walter Toman's birth order schema. It is not as much used as it once was, but it is still kind of fun to use. I'm almost sure that my approach included an exploration of her family system, with Murray Bowen and his disciples' emphasis on families as systems in mind.

As I'm writing this in 2020, the issue of 'unconscious bias' is very prominent. Forty years ago, the bias was surely a reality no less than it is today, but it was clearly—at least for me then—more unconscious.

So I'm even now embarrassed to recall that at some point in the interview I asked her something about whether working in a largely white institution would be a problem for her.

She bristled. "Would you ask a white student such a question?"

I'd like to claim that I had the wisdom and the humility to acknowledge the racism inherent in my question, but I didn't. I was so taken aback that I mumbled a denial.

Obviously, that event remains in my memory. Even now I wish I had been able to commend her for her willingness to confront me. What a remarkable possibility might have opened to both of us—a courageous young woman and a supervisor willing to learn. Alas, it wasn't to be.

I clearly failed that day to practice what I hope every good Chaplain incorporates in his practice, namely the ability to self-reflect and self-supervise in the moment. My non-anxious self had absconded.

One lesson I learn and re-learn, usually after the fact, is that one crucial pastoral strategy is: *pause! Always* take a moment before responding. I have regretted it every time I have failed to pause.

Chapter 19

JERRY AND THEOLOGICAL REFLECTION IN CPE

ALL CPE PROGRAMS INCLUDE in their curriculum some form of what we call "theological reflection". Years ago, when I began as a CPE Supervisor, the matter of what we mean when we say "God" did not evoke much of a question for me or the students. That is, the existence of God—with a capital G—was assumed. But how to characterize 'him' (the gender was not questioned) and what it might mean to invoke him in prayer, and what we might expect of him— these were all legitimate areas of inquiry in the reflection/evaluation portion of the verbatim document. Legitimate also is a consideration of the nature and extent of the patient's belief system. Of course, in any honest conversation, the wonderment about the very existence and nature of God lurked; how could it not in the setting where most CPE programs locate—in the setting in which Chaplains encounter patients and nurses and doctors at cross-purposes with each other, sometimes angrily; in which student Chaplains begin to clash with one another and their teacher, sometimes angrily; in which disease and death, often utimely, invades the clinic, sometimes angrily.

So, what do we mean by theological reflection? Maybe more to the point of this book, how does the supervisor/educator use his own process of inquiring/reflecting on the nature of a God who seems to allow a world that appears to encompass both good and evil?

In Chapter 23 I have more to say about "doing" theology.

So many years ago that the details are hazy to me, there was a student in one of the Resident groups in my early years in Knoxville. He was big and friendly and a bit blustery, and, withal, I remember him as, initially, a good student. I'll call him "Jerry". One of the ways I try to nudge my students toward seeing god's humanity and the beauty in that humanity—in all the human stuff we experience from day to day—is to introduce them to some of the stuff through novels. There was a particular novel, *The House of God*, by Samuel Shem, which I liked. I appreciated the novel's realistic portrayal of the education of medical Residents; as a way to cope with the stresses and strains of their work and education they are depicted as profane, irreverent, and morally loose. The novel is both serious and comic. Since the Chaplain Residents inhabit this same world, my thought is that reading this novel is a relatively gentle way to expand the student's view of God and those who inhabit God's world.

Jerry must have gotten far enough into the novel to read about the loose sexual couplings and the irreverent ways the Residents spoke about their dying patients to realize the sharp contrast between his rigid fundamentalist religious perspective and the behavior described in the book —Jerry's God does not countenance such behavior. He refused to read the novel, which had the unfortunate consequence that he failed to get the major message delivered by the protagonist, the fat man, as valid for Pastoral as for Medical Residents: that we do the best for our patients when we do the least. Somehow this refusal became total resistance to participating in the program. Finally, I had to dismiss him.

I do not recount this with any pride. I still resist acknowledging my own rigidity. And I wonder to myself, would my mellower—and, hopefully, more mature—self have found a way to back off from this confrontation and a gentler way to face him into his own insistence on a god who is only righteous and pure and in whom is no room for acceptance of human faults. If I had trusted more in our own CPE credo, to trust the process, might I have found a way to use my own rigidity to sit along-side him in his, thus demonstrating the value in sharing human limitations?

Perhaps there is at least one more thing to say about the place of theological reflection in CPE. Tangentially, but not unimportantly, the power dynamic is a factor. I am the teacher! My own theological view has broadened over the years. So a major question is, how can the I as the educator both encourage students to widen their theological field of vision and yet honor the field where they currently dwell.[1] Put another way, I believe that each student's religion is both broader and deeper than any verbalization can capture, so to honor that religion as Paul did ("It is plain to see that you Athenians take your religion seriously . . . ") is my first task, before any attempt to expand their theology. Encounters with patients, families and fellow staff members—especially members of the peer group—is usually enough to challenge a "narrow" theological view. Maybe Jerry and I could have found another way to approach the broadening task.

As it was, we escorted him out of the building. I have no idea what became of him. But I do have the hope—even the conviction—that he has been offered many more opportunities to experience the grace in the acceptance of his own humanity.

As I have been.

---

1. I am reminded of Rumi's famous poem that begins with *"Out beyond ideas of wrongdoing and rightdoing, there is a field. I'll meet you there . . . "* I encourage you to read the complete poem.

Chapter 20

LENA

LENA WALKED INTO MY OFFICE. This was so long ago that I can no longer remember whether this was her first week as a Chaplain Resident or was an Admission interview. I do remember that her walk was somewhat awkward, since she had braces on each leg.

Her speech, as well as her walk, was a little bit "spastic"; this term may sound disparaging and dismissive, but I mean it here to be only descriptive. "Spastic", in fact, is how CP—cerebral palsy— is described in the literature.

Lena was quite open about the fact that she has CP. "I tend to have seizures", she said, and, forthwith and immediately, gave me a demonstration—she had a seizure right there in my office at our very first meeting!

Panic? Not quite; I didn't have time to panic. The seizure was over as quickly as it began. As the year wore on, her seizures often took the form of what I thought of then as a fugue state. I have since learned that is an incorrect label and that what she was having was an "absence seizure". You might usually not even notice, unless you were paying direct close attention. She would just be "gone" from 20-30 seconds and then fully back with me/us.

Her peers and I soon learned to notice when she left us and to take a short pause until she returned.

Lena seemed initially to be a bit childlike, and there was a sweetness to her. Over time I also came to appreciate that she was very bright. She was also not above using her seizures to get people to treat her gently even when she might have needed to be pushed about her work. Part of her charm was that she was quite open with her manipulativeness—she knew she used her CP, and she would quite freely acknowledge that. She would laugh when we called her on that; and she would agree.

My feeling memory of her is positive, but the facts are hazy; I have the sense that she was a good learner and that she made good use of her time with us learning to practice the art of pastoral care. Those she worked with gave good reports. Lena was more than competent as a Chaplain.

Occasionally, as now, Lena comes to mind, though she was a student in my early days at Duke—forty some years ago. I wish I had kept notes; I wish I could report something of the specifics of her work as a developing minister, but, alas, I have told you what I remember of her—a happy memory.

I do still feel gratitude that she was willing to push herself to participate in a rigorous year of training in the clinic and that she offered me and her colleagues the opportunity to learn to see and to appreciate the value and the beauty—and the *capacities*—of what we now call "differently-abled" people.

Chapter 21

POETRY AND METAPHOR

MY FATHER, LONG SINCE departed this life, still comes to mind from time to time. I still miss him and find myself wishing I could talk to him.

In a way, I still think of him as a no-nonsense business man. He worked hard and he prospered—not a lot of poetry in his soul, or so, if I'd had the language for it then, I might have thought.

His offspring, my siblings and I, all seem to me to be somewhat like him in that way—hardworking, serious and no-nonsense. I don't think of myself as very open to or appreciative of poetry—I just don't get it. I suspect that my siblings, also, would tend more toward being like engineers than like poets; *pace* engineers; I mean no disrespect.

And yet, my father was extremely generous with his money and his time; maybe I didn't know this side of him, because he didn't talk much about himself as a generous person or about his emotional self. In retrospect it may be fair to say that he was very loving but not, for whatever reason, good at verbalizing it. But I do know that he loved good music, mostly classical. He could get very emotional as he listened to a Beethoven symphony, for example; he clearly deeply enjoyed it—surely an indication of poetry in his soul.

I don't easily appreciate written poetry, and I can easily miss the beauty all around me. But I think that one of the ways I feel still connected to my father is that music, in many varieties— Handel's Hallelujah Chorus or Leonard Cohen's Hallelujah or a Willie Nelson ballad, for example—cause my tears to well up and overwhelm me with joy and beyond; that may be my poetic sensibility.

It occurs to me that one way to understand my long-time interest in CPE is to note its emphasis on attending to feelings, to the a-rational components of a person's response to the world around her. And it seems to me that it is my attempt to correct my limitation as a CPE Educator which is based in my lack of fluency in the language of poetry. And I do mean lack of fluency, not lack of poetry in my soul.

I think of poetry and metaphor in the same way. And I like to believe that metaphor and poetry are really the preferred language of the common "man". That is, when she says, "God told me", a literalist might imagine a Being giving a specific and unambiguous directive; but left to her own natural instincts the common woman knows she is speaking of her sense that she is being guided; that the world can generally be understood to offer potential guidance —sometimes gentle, sometimes harsh—through life's normal but hardly definable realities. A chance encounter, or word, or normally unremarkable event suddenly gets her attention in a new way— "did not our hearts burn within us?"[1] The literalists among us might be comfortable seeing the conversation between God and Moses at the burning bush as an actual historical event, but we can just as easily trust God at work by suddenly sensing that normally unremarkable event as having new and deeper significance.

Richard Rohr, in a recent (March 24, 2021) daily meditation notes that a famous 20th century Rabbi, Abraham Heschel, sees the Biblical prophets as poets, "gifted with creativity and imagination. What the poets know as poetic inspiration, the prophets call divine revelation . . . The inspiration of the artist is what is meant by 'the hand of the Lord which rests upon the prophet' . . . a poet, he is endowed with sensibility, enthusiasm, and tenderness, and above all, with a way of thinking imaginatively".

What a liberating reality! The world is too rich to be bound by a literal interpretation. I have been alerted to this richness many times and in many ways over the years. A seminal book for me was Sallie McFague's *Metaphorical Theology*. The engineer's attention to the measure of things is not at all unimportant, but, like many logically minded,

1. Luke 24:32

rational-dependent (often described as left-brained) people, I can easily miss the less measurable, more free-flow of life. I am not the first to note that, even though measuring is important, not everything that is measured is important, and, conversely, not everything that is important can be measured.

Maybe a really good way to think about CPE is to see it as teaching pastors to read their parishioners as poetry.

It also occurs to me that it is not too great a stretch to say that I appreciate God's —or the great spirit of the universe's—good humor and great wisdom in getting me together with Helen, the artist.

Chapter 22

GOD KEEPS DYING

(a light-hearted attempt at theologizing)

WOE IS ME. Today Carl Jung and Edwin Reischauer died.

Carl is widely known, Reischauer probably less so.

A friend recently mentioned a book she had been reading having to do with the development of Jung's theories. I was interested, and she kindly gave it to me to read: *Toni Wolff & C.G. Jung; A Collaboration*[1]. I am in no sense a Jungian scholar; but I do have some interest and some limited knowledge with an appreciation for Jung's 'spiritual' approach. His concepts like 'individuation' and 'shadow' and types and archetypes all seemed to make sense and to be useful to anyone, like clergy or analysts, or social workers, who work with people. What intrigued me, though, was Toni Wolff; I had never heard her name before.

The book was not well written, but the material was powerfully captivating. According to the author, much of what we think we know about Jung and his theories would not even exist without the collaboration of Toni Wolff. It was she who helped him shape and come to understand for himself his developing understanding of humanity and psychoanalysis. She was his handmaid, his muse, the *anima* to his *animus*. Without her, at least as Dr. Healy tells it, we would likely not have Jungian analysis.

1. Healy, Nan Savage

Carl Jung had been near the top of my pantheon. In an article given to me in the early 70's by my mentor at Vanderbilt, entitled "Psychotherapy or the Clergy", Jung briefly and brilliantly makes the point that each of us has to come to terms with the 'dark' side, the shadow, residing in us: if we cannot love that one, we cannot love another. I was particularly drawn to his very imaginative biblical allusion.[2]

So to read of his shabby treatment of Toni, of his denial of her central importance both in his life and his work, has taken him down from the pedestal I had for him. He's just another man, massively dependent on the woman and massively resistant to acknowledging it—a woman he uses up and then discards. No god there. (Or, maybe, a dark and cruel one.) One down.

One of the most popular courses at Harvard in the fifties, one we irreverently and non- politically correctly called "rice-paddies", was taught by two stars in Harvard's constellation of professors, John K. Fairbank (China) and Edwin O. Reischauer (Japan). The lecture hall was large and always jammed full with undergraduates.

In those days, Reischauer was the unquestioned expert about all things Japanese. His thesis has been dominant for the last 60 or so years, the thesis being that Japan has been in process of "Westernizing" itself over the last two or three centuries. In the on-line Magazine, *Aeon* (2/9/21), is a brief and well-written article by Professor Jon Davidann (Hawai'i Pacific University). The professor asserts that Reischauer's basic theme is pure fiction—a product of a westerner's imagination. The professor persuasively demolishes the thesis of Japanese westernization. From his well-documented recounting of the situation, it is clear that the Japanese were always resistant to the many dangers they saw in western culture. Professor Davidann has declared that God Reischauer is dead. Two down.

A while ago, my very skeptical younger brother, Tim, sent me a video clip of a brief conversation between comedian and writer, Ricky Gervais, and television show host, Stephen Colbert. In it Gervais is asserting

2. *What I do unto the least of my brethren, that I do unto Christ. But what if I should discover that the least amongst them all, the poorest of all beggars, the most impudent of all offenders, yea the very fiend himself that these are within me, and that I myself stand in need of the alms of my own kindness, that I myself am the enemy who must be loved what then?*

that God doesn't exist. Actually, he makes the agnostic argument very briefly, namely, that Colbert can't prove that God exists and that there are other explanations for everything that is that make more reasonable sense. Tim sent the clip to family members as a clear expression of his own position. God is not only dead; he never lived! Three down.

Poor God. Feet of clay; massively biased; maybe no feet at all.

Every time I begin to think I have a fix on something, that's there some certain solid ground, I discover that that very God I had put my hopes in is dead.

Reminds me of the title of a lecture I once heard about: "Everything nailed down is coming loose".

Is there but one conclusion left to us? Is it that the untold number of people who continue to believe that God is are simply deluded?

Or might it be possible that it is the God whose name is rationality is dead? Maybe God does not live in the hard wind of rationality or the omniscient power of the earthquake or the logic of the fire; maybe God is in the "sound of sheer silence".[3]

Maybe God can't be defined; maybe God can't be understood; maybe God can't be known . . .

Well then, what good is (s)he?

Who knows?

With Iris Dement[4], I think *"I'll just let the mystery be"*.

---

3. 1 Kings, 19:11—12
4. And, if you don't know her, you might want to find this song on YouTube

Chapter 23

My Theology

MAYBE THE PREVIOUS TWO CHAPTERS are all that is needed by way of theology, but the engineer in me has this additional commentary, illustrating doing theology.

I really mean by the title of this chapter to refer to my *current* theological stance since, like the weather, my understanding is subject to change (once again, "trust the process").

Earlier I mentioned theological reflection but that Chapter (19) was mostly about how I was trying to help Jerry expand what I saw as his limited and restricted theological (and, therefore, pastoral) stance.

One other thing I need to note right away is that CPE, in its particularity, expects students to attend to their own cultural background and history, including especially its religious component, and how that affects their theological perspective. Understanding that heritage makes it available to them as part of their equipment for pastoring.

I speak, think, write from within my culture—such an obvious statement when you think about it. How can any one of us do otherwise? But we are intentional about attending to it, since it is so much a part of us that it can easily be taken for granted and so its impact can remain unexamined and unavailable for our use. Anyhow, one important component of my enculturation is Christianity including its Jewish roots— my version of Christianity as shaped by the Episcopal Church.

So now to theology, which has something to do with 'god and related subjects', as one of my favorite professors used to say.

True to CPE's attention to the specifics of the clinical moment, usually what we ask of the student is to reflect on the theology inherent in the particular encounter she is reporting. We mean to ask the presenter what s/he thinks and means when using or excluding the term "God"; and we are also interested to know what the patient means—whether using God language or not. And then we want to know in what way, if any, God is thought to be and/or experienced as present in the encounter. And this also likely involves an issue already mentioned in earlier chapters, namely authority; by identifying as Chaplain what does s/he think she is claiming or representing? Is she only speaking of God's presence, or is she being God's presence?

Now that term, "being God's presence" suggests a theological concept—incarnation. I don't know that Christianity "owns" that concept, but it commonly refers, in traditional Christian understanding, to Jesus as God in human flesh.

But that can be a problem. I mean, for example, that while Jews and Muslims believe in Jesus as prophet and teacher, (but not savior) as well as in the possibility of God's manifesting God's self in human form, popular Christianity claims that it is Jesus alone who incarnates God—that Jesus is somehow uniquely God. Many Christians seem to believe that John's Gospel (14:6): "I am the way and the truth and the life. No one comes to the Father except through me"—is literally true: there is only one way and it is our way, in the current phrase, or the highway.

The exclusivity of that perspective is theologically suspect and pastorally destructive.

But, as I noted in Chapter 21, if we read John as poetry, as speaking metaphorically, then we can celebrate Jesus as an expression of a universal truth—descriptive of a reality that transcends Judaism, Islam, Christianity or any other religion (and, perhaps, even any non-religious system or philosophy). I think that all the 'major religions' think of Jesus as in some way or another reflective or representative of God, so that if we Christians can bring ourselves to give up our exclusive claim, we can all live in a more spacious and hospitable world. A more gracious Christianity celebrates the presence of God in each human.

A useful way to think of the stories about Jesus is as fairy tales or myths (in the best sense of those terms as conveying truth through a story). So, for example, the stories we have—as amended by me in my reading and telling—picture a man who is accepted by his friends as their leader. The stories picture a gang, men and women, people who like to get together and go fishing and have a beer and a fish fry on the beach and enjoy life. They picture a man who likes to tell stories and tease his friends with riddles. They picture a man who seems to make friends widely beyond the little gang and with all sorts of people. This picture might get a little complicated here, since Jesus seems to befriend people that his friends don't normally associate with. Further, he sometimes astounds them by appearing to cure afflictions and miraculously feed people; and by some of the outrageous things he says. In short, with all these imagined aspects, this story conveys a picture of one who is his own man, a man, who embraces life —all of life—fully. And we do know enough to be pretty sure that there was something about him that drew people to him—people loved him. There were also some who hated him.

Now you might be thinking, Peter, you are just making up stories about Jesus.

Well, yes. And I would add that this is what humans always do, corporately and individually. The Church has always made up Jesus. But not out of whole cloth; there really was a man Jesus[1] who made enough of an impression that stories about what he did and said were recalled and later written down; I've just used my imagination to expand on what his every-day life might have looked like, beyond the dramatic high points.

So this representative-of-god man both *tells* stories, *and* (as with each of us) his life *is* a story. He is a model, as have been many others, of what it looks like when a person deliberately lives as if God dwells in them, as if incarnation is true. The story of his life allows us to see that each life has its uniqueness, yet with common characteristics: each begins in its own peculiar and special circumstances, each inevitably includes joy and pain, delight and suffering, *and each ends in death*. (See Chapter 30 on this.) Jesus as model embraces all of his joy and sorrow in all of its

---

1. Bart Ehrman teaches religion at UNC Chapel Hill, NC; he is a scholar who has studied religion and Christianity deeply. He is convinced and convincing that there was a historical man named Jesus who lived at the time and in the place described in the Gospels.

particularities. And, being a good Jew, that includes his embrace of the belief that God dwells in him—that he is the son of man (*ben adam*). When Christianity understands itself to be speaking poetically, it makes sense to get that, as the one in whom god dwells, he takes on all the ills (or, if you insist, the sins) of the world. And so do we.

Other people put it differently, without any reference to Jesus, but they say the same thing when they declare that "life is hard". You don't have to believe in Jesus to wrestle with that reality and with the question as to whether and how much you will *embrace all of life* fully or how you will try to *avoid living* (also referenced in Chapter 30). Jesus lives out that struggle: "I'd rather not suffer this death" he said, "but I know this is how it is; so I say, yes, I'll do it."

Popular Christianity suffers from *the basic heresy* (see Chapter 13) of believing in either/or—believing that you can have, or be, one or the other, but not both. (And recall the parable of Rabbi Moishe in that same chapter.) In particular, popular Christianity speaks of heaven and hell, of Jesus as "overcoming sin", sin being evil and evil needing to be overcome, or taken away or abolished. The problem we all face, of course, is that it is the nature of human nature to include both good and bad impulses, thoughts, feelings. In his March 30, 2021 meditation, Richard Rohr says this:

"The mystery of the cross teaches us how to stand against hate without becoming hate, how to oppose evil without becoming evil ourselves."

My immediate thought was and is that Rohr can't quite seem to bring himself to fully embrace, as I believe is our only option, the reality of our unity, our oneness. Put simply, we *are* hate (*and* love); we *are* evil (*and* good). In a separate piece I wrote recently I suggested that we might think of God as both good and evil and as so much more that he comprehends both.

Sin is as vital to us as our heart. The notion of cutting sin out of our lives recalls to me that sad old joke about the surgeon reporting to the patient's family, 'the surgery was successful, but the patient died'. Better that we should learn to live with a diseased heart.

The downside of religion—or, to be fair, more accurately of the religion I know best—is that it always wants to abolish sin rather than to embrace it. I quoted Carl Jung's notion in footnote 2, page 73. And I mean that if we are not either/or but both/and, then rather than trying to overcome or abolish sin, we can and must embrace it. If God is big enough to comprehend—that is, to embrace—both good and evil, that is the model for us. Jesus models in the drama of his story what it means to live with integrity—to accept all that life brings, including all its ills and its end.

The Christian formula is that Jesus is fully human and at the same time, without sin. Now that is just a logical impossibility! To be human, by definition, is to be sinful; or, in other words, flawed—less than perfect. So what are we to do? We could recall Lao Tzu: "Do you want to improve the world? It can't be done; it is perfect as it is". In other words, the logical contradiction gets overcome by the notion that human being— i.e. sinful human being—is perfection. "God" (or "being itself" or "the ground of being", as Paul Tillich put it) fully embraces and comprehends (or, if you prefer, forgives=accepts without reservation) humans.

Richard Rohr also appreciates Julian of Norwich, and notes in another meditation that "[Dame Julian] insists on the marriage of nature and God, on panentheism [God in all things and all things in God] as the very meaning of faith, and on the marriage of God and the human (for we, too, are part of nature): 'between God and the human there is no between'. . ."

Which may bring us back to earth, so to speak—to the earth that the Chaplain treads daily. She will meet people so like herself that, if she will allow it, she will know them intimately. She and they will be wrestling with this very same reality: even with all its joys, life is hard; how can I face it? Must I?

I will chastise her if she reports to me that she introduced God to her patient—God as a noun. And I will praise her if she knows that God is a verb and speaks 'God' only when that is the language comfortable to her patient.

In an earlier iteration of this chapter, I had included a section on theodicy (how can a good god allow bad things?), but I realize that would be superfluous, since God's "message", exhibited everywhere, all the time, and in all things, animate and inanimate, is that life is beautiful, flawed, perfect, imperfect, joyful, hard; that death is inevitable. Jesus is a model, though not the only one, of accepting his lot, knowing that it meant accepting the death that mysteriously incorporates, includes, and continues life.

Can I—can my student—model acceptance for the patient?

Chapter 24

THE GRACIOUS RABBI

HE AND I SERVED together on the Board of the ACPE years ago.

He was a Rabbi (in the Orthodox tradition, if I remember rightly); he was not reticent to speak his mind.

I think perceived him as a bit arrogant initially; as is often the case, what I later had to acknowledge was that the arrogance was mine (can you say "projection"?)

His refusal to use the term "god" seemed to me then to be a silly literalist convention. I mean he would refer to g*d, but refuse to put the "o" in.

Luckily, or arrogantly, or foolishly, one day during a break in our meeting, I risked a direct confrontation: "you're just playing a game by leaving out the letter "o"; I don't understand that".

I don't remember what his response was, but I do remember that he was gracious. The result was that he who for me had been a strange other became a friend and colleague. Not a big risk, perhaps, but I did run the risk of making an enemy; instead, by his kindness, he became a friend. Once again, I learned the importance and the value, of daring to risk.

In fact, as I will say in more detail in the next chapter, one way to describe a core element of CPE is that it is about practicing risky interpersonal behavior.

Years later, during which time my theological perspective had continued to change and, so I hope, become more gracious, I encountered him at one of our annual meetings. I told him that I had never forgotten my confrontation of him years ago and I thanked him for his patience with me. And I told him I wanted to apologize, that I had come to appreciate his perspective that the reason he refused to name the one is that g*d is too big to be limited by any name.

Again, he was gracious.

Just then another friend came up to us and asked what we were talking about. There was a moment of silence; how to tell that we were talking about what cannot be named? Then I said, "I can't say". And my Rabbi friend and I laughed out loud.

So, two points here: one is the simple and profound theological notion of the vastness of the reality that most religionists dare to limit with the name "god"—a continuing theme throughout this book.

The other is the matter of risk, to which I devote the next chapter.

Chapter 25

Risk

RECENTLY I HELPED WITH an admission interview (into a Chaplain Residency program). The applicant seemed to me to be difficult to make personal contact with. Her response to several invitations to give us something of the particulars of herself, her person, was to give impersonal and general replies. After some time, and in order to see how she might handle a more direct attempt to meet her, I simply told her that I was having trouble making contact with her. Since CPE is about enhancing the student's ability to make contact with fellow humans, and since the clinic where that is practiced includes plenty of direct confrontation, it makes sense to give the interviewee a sample of the kind and flavor of work that she will be engaging in, including reflecting on her encounters and the feeling evoked in her by them. I was heartened for a moment by her silence following my confrontation; perhaps she could share what my confrontation evoked in her. But it didn't happen. Since my colleague in the interview process tends to be a bit gentler than I, I knew I could count on him to invite her to reflect, as the interview was concluding, on her overall experience of the interview. She was able to acknowledge some anxiety but nothing else. After the interviewee left the room, he and I agreed that she seemed to us to be a rather weak candidate by reason of her difficulty with engaging.

We in CPE know that we need not artificially "inject" troubling issues or risk into the learning environment. We know—and trust— that the environment provides all of that by its very nature. Meeting with patients, family members, staff members, peers, bosses, all are occasions fraught with both the possibility of warm meeting and of troubling conflict and of deep pain and grief. Every meeting with another of this human race holds that promise and risk. What CPE does need always to do is to practice dealing with those inevitable conflicts, problems, risks and promises—learning to confront the 'hard things' head on. Both the clinic where patients, families, staff are and the clinic of the peer group, provide the arenas where these confrontations and conflicts may happen. The Educator doesn't make it happen, and she does not create the fire, though she may fan the flames and stir the pot occasionally.

Seminaries may teach the theory that life entails risk; CPE requires students to enter that life of risking real personal contact with "strangers".

It is hard for me to realize that I began my CPE career not too long after the Association was first formed in 1967. Which is to say that I have lived in and absorbed much of the lore of our Association as it has grown and changed. CPE had, of course, been in existence as an educational process long before its formal organization, so the lore includes stories about our founding mothers and fathers.

One bit of the persistent lore throughout our history has been the "war stories" told by one generation of CPE students to the next. Each new group of summer Interns would let me know sometime during the summer that they had heard how tough CPE was. They heard that supervisors would attack your theological beliefs and give harsh judgments about your work with patients; that CPE was a sort of "boot camp" that only the tough could survive, that here was deep exploration of your own psychological makeup which was not always gently done.

How much those stories reflect the reality of CPE as practiced is surely subject to question, but the stories seem to have a life of their own. And, of course, they are not the only stories and reactions people have about their CPE experience. Year after year students report that the experience has been positive and life-changing precisely because of the challenges and the self-exploration. They were glad to have been provided the opportunity to meet people in extreme situations, strangers with whom they were expected to make significant contact and to whom they were expected to offer pastoral (often now called spiritual) care. Further sharing their work with a small group of other strangers whose job was to criticize that work, while sometimes anxiety producing, also became a supportive learning experience. It is a risky business that promises great reward.

Many programs expected students to take turns serving on-call overnight, usually "in house".

But, other than fatigue, there was not much physical danger that Chaplains needed to fear. It was the more inter-and intra-personal matters that seemed risky. Meeting a patient whose religious perspective was so apparently different from my own posed its own challenge to my belief system and, maybe more importantly, to my sense of myself, my self-esteem; and subjecting my work and my theology to scrutiny and criticism by peers and supervisor carries its own kind of psychological risk.

Over the years, both from internal pressure (to monitor ourselves carefully) and external (we live in an age currently, when rightly or wrongly, many students feel unsafe), ACPE Educators have, as best I can tell, generally tended toward being less confronting, and they have become deliberate in working to provide a safe and supportive atmosphere. These are good and admirable impulses. However, the tendency seems to be to demand less of students: fewer hours, compensatory time when on call, gentle, nonconfronting evaluations that emphasize only positive attributes and avoid naming anything judged to be negative, and avoidance of conflict—in short, anything that feels unsafe to the student. As I write this in mid-2021, the mood in the administration and professor ranks in academia is decidedly cautious: it has become commonplace to warn students that they might be exposed to unsetting material. This is called "trigger warnings". The academy feels the need to provide students safe spaces and to avoid risk.

To focus on safety to the exclusion of risk is theologically and educationally unsound. We know that Abraham is promised a good land as his destination, and we know the story—we know that the journey is fraught with danger and hardships.

Not every encounter a pastor has with a patient or a parishioner is conflict free. And it is surely the case that the intensive and close work in a small group will generate conflict. Which is to say that to encounter the micro- or the macro-world is to face conflict. We do not serve our students well if, in the guise of keeping them safe, we do not acknowledge the conflict and practice ways to deal with it. Personal, pastoral authority gets honed when the student encounters it in her supervisor (either by resisting or accepting) and in herself when it is resisted or accepted in her by the patient or parishioner.

The "war stories" vastly distort the picture of life in a CPE program, but, as with the interviewee at the beginning of this chapter, it would be malpractice on our part to deny the reality of the risks involved. The initial interview itself is, in an important sense, the "trigger warning".

It occurs to me that, in addition, a statement in the "contract for learning" which students are to sign as they begin might repeat that the work is hard, challenging, and demanding of time and energy and may involve interpersonal conflict. "Fair warning", the auctioneer calls out just before he brings the hammer down to close the sale.

Chapter 26

THE GROUP

ONE OF MY COLLEAGUES who read some of this noted that I had said little about the group life.

And he is right.

Now CPE distinguishes between "Level I" and "Level II". Years ago, CPE designated "Basic" and "Advanced" CPE. True to my resistance to rigid distinctions and definitions, I had been successful in convincing our organization to do away with those categories; only to see them return in their current guise. I certainly don't disagree that beginning CPE (usually the first Unit) tends to focus, as we did in the group I began writing about, on the person of the pastor and his sense of authority; while a year-long program (usually three or four consecutive Units) will expand the focus to include the many other aspects of pastoral practice—e.g., personality and systems theories; special characteristics of various "diagnoses" in the population bring served, etc. Yet I continue to insist that I and we all are always in the process of growing, the process that always includes regression and progression. As some days I'm a beginner and some days I'm the most accomplished Pastor/Chaplain who has ever been, so with each and every one of us. As my friend, Steve, says, "if you haven't fouled, it is only because you haven't been in the game."

Which is, perhaps a long way, to say that it surely goes without saying that *the context* in which personal development can take place is invariably the group, the community, the (little "c") church.

As much as I caution against rigid adherence to any specific theoretical frame, it should be clear that exposure to a variety of frames can only enhance and expand the student's horizon on relationships. So the groups I work with typically do some reading on group processes and on systems; I will typically present what CPE has traditionally called "didactics" on these and other theories (such as personality theories). And our group meetings also included a case presentation seminar (almost always the presentation was in verbatim form), and what I call an open agenda seminar, in which any matter might be a topic for discussion with the intent always to attend to how the members were relating to one another. Each seminar was always one and a half hours long.

What follows is what an "Open Agenda" Seminar in a first Unit might look like. Some people label such a meeting an IPR (Interpersonal Relations Seminar), because the intent is both to attend to both the reality that each of us is an individual 'agent; and that we are always formed and forming in community. I usually call it "Open Agenda" to imply that subject matter is not predetermined, but I am open with the students about the fact that we will be attending to interpersonal relations and to systems and group process, whatever "subject" is being discussed.

The participants in this group are: Mary, young, Methodist, Black, not married, seminarian, cute, energetic; Carl, middle-age, white, Southern Baptist Minister, divorced, recently resigned from his pastorate because he had an affair, quiet, thoughtful; Ginger, in her 40's, Episcopal Deacon, white, overweight, not married, serving in a local church, pleasant, somewhat guarded; Timothy, late twenties, Southern Baptist Pastor, white, married, two children, quite conservative theologically. Isabel, 35, married with one child, in Rabbinical (reformed) school, bright, assertive.

This is a summer Unit, a single Unit, and this is the first CPE experience for all except Carl who had completed a Unit years ago; for him this current Unit is preparatory to his entering a year-long Chaplain Residency program. This open agenda session was four weeks into the 11-week summer Unit. The group is beginning to get beyond typical beginning group caution and "politeness".

Mary 1: (*cheerily*) Good morning everybody! How are you today?

Ginger 1: Oh, not so good . . . I had a really rough on-call last night and I'm tired. That man in the ICU who's been trying to die, finally did last night. It was a nightmare. The family was hysterical . . . They . . .

Isabel 1: (*cutting in, sharply*) I don't like it when you talk like that – 'trying to die' – that sounds so disrespectful!

Ginger 2:(*retreating, softly*) Oh, I'm so sorry; I didn't mean to offend you.

Mary 2: Oh, come on, Isabel, she's just letting off a little steam; lighten up.

Isabel 2: Listen, I have a right to say what I feel as much as you do.

Mary starts to respond, but,

Carl 1: Let's all ease up a little, friends, we don't need to fight.

Isabel 3: Well, maybe we do; you know, Carl, if you were a better fighter you might not have had to divorce.

Ginger 3: Now wait a minute, Isabel; that's pretty harsh.

Timothy 1: The Bible says not to judge unless you be also judged. Sure is a lot of judging going on here.

It looks like Mary is about to respond to Timothy, but . . .

Carl 2: Isabel, that hurt! But, you know, maybe you're right. I'll have to think about that.

Timothy 2: but Carl, maybe all you need to do is confess your sins; I mean, adultery . . . I don't know how you can even be a pastor . . .

Mary 3: Talk about judging!! I'm tired of your Baptist piety!

(I'm pleased that they are engaging one another; typical of a beginning group, they have tended to be gentle with one another and to avoid "hot" topics. Isabel has tended to be the provocateur in the group, but the others have usually done like Ginger did at first – back away. Isabel has pushed several times before; and Mary and Timothy have sparred from time to time, but Carl and Ginger have, usually successfully, tried to calm troubled waters. The issue for me at this moment is when to intervene to ask for them to reflect on the group's process. I'd begin with, how are you feeling right at this moment? And I'd focus on questions like, what feelings did you bring in today? what feelings got stirred? And I'd also then invite them to think about this group as a system – we have studied family systems – so to talk about how the various parts of the system are acting and reacting; if there are some issues being named openly today that have not been, what was preventing their open appearance before today; and how did the group (as system) decide to bring them out today? Finally I would hope to get them to see the connection between their engaging in this way with each other and the kinds of family engaging that Ginger mentioned as the meeting began).

In the early weeks of the Unit I mean to be the 'process observer/commentator' with the intent of modeling attention to the process. As the students grow into the Unit, they will take on this work for themselves and each other.

So back to the group:

> Peter 1: Well, Isabel, you finally got what you've been after, eh?
>
> Isabel 4: Why, Peter, I don't know what you mean (she *smiles broadly*)
>
> Peter 2: Carl, do you believe that Isabel doesn't know what she's doing?
>
> Carl 3: Not for a minute. Isabel, I think maybe you can teach me some things.

Indirection and playfulness. I refer to what the group knows but hasn't directly addressed—Isabel's assertiveness and that she risked moving to a deeper level with Carl. Rather than directly naming the action, I prefer to play and that way to encourage them to continue, trusting that the other group members will get drawn into deeper waters, too. So I'm *not* confronting them here; I don't need to, Isabel and Carl have engaged; I just affirm it.

There are two family therapists who come to mind here, Carl Whitaker (his book, with Gus Napier, is *The Family Crucible*), and Edwin Friedman (*Generation to Generation*). Each of them takes their work with families seriously but both use humor and are quite playful in their interactions with family members. Friedman explained that his intent is to indicate *both* that he is there with them, that is, he hears the seriousness of the concern, *and* that, even though he knows the issue is serious, he will not be overwhelmed, he will maintain calm, be the "non-anxious presence"—another instance of "this is you and this is me".

> Mary 4: This group may be fun! And I sure need to get into it with you, Timothy.

> Ginger 4: I didn't mean to call you 'harsh' Isabel; please forgive me.

This is more than enough to illustrate how a group might go. I admit to getting a little idealistic here at the end of this imagined group meeting. Imagining Mary getting into the 'play' this quickly might be a little unrealistic; and I just had fun having Ginger retreat so obviously. In time the hope is that she will go from gingerly to ginger.

I don't necessarily want Ginger and Isabel to fight, but I do want them to attend to the unspoken in relationships; I do want them to learn to read the signals so that they can more fully and realistically make contact (or not, as circumstances suggest) with a peer, a spouse, a patient.

> Peter 3: So, Ginger, might you consider what you hoped to accomplish by apologizing to Isabel?

So the beat goes on . . .

Some years ago, I was delighted to discover that the word "nice" derives from two Latin words, *ne* = not, and *scire* = to know; and I delight to share that information with my students early in our time together.

Surely it is clear from my commentary that I think learning how to confront and learning how to be direct with one another is crucial for good pastoral care. The word "confront" is often heard and felt as negative, but it doesn't have to be; I mean it to be more neutrally understood as facing directly into. In working with the clinical material students bring, I try to model confrontation as sensitive and appropriate and sometimes direct and sometimes indirect. Recall, for example, that in Chapter 2 I told Lou that I didn't like his God; in context, that was a clear and direct message; Lou got it! Conversations between Pastor and Patient often begin like conversations in a beginning Open Agenda group—cautiously—the participants feeling each other out. In time, sometimes quickly and sometimes slowly, the participants begin to go deeper with one another—parallel process yet again. The group meeting is another clinic where we learn by practicing how to connect with one another. The bedside is where it all happens.

One thing that many CPE Supervisors of my era did was to seek also some certification as a Pastoral Counselor, usually with the American Association of Pastoral Counselors (mentioned above in Chapter 1). I often had a limited practice as a Pastoral Counselor throughout my career. When people came to see me as counselor I would always find a way to explore with them their "fight styles". Many assured me that they did not fight! Uh Huh! That's sort of like secrets. I used to tell students and counselees that every family or system has secrets. And I would follow that with, there's no such thing as a secret. What I mean by all of that is that secrets are simply those matters that every one agrees, verbally or not, not to talk about. It is the same with fighting. Conflicts, disagreements will happen between two people, particularly if they've been together for some time, as in married. The question is, how will they handle those conflicts. It is common knowledge that when a sweet southern lady wants to express her disapproval of another person without an open conflict, she will say "Bless her heart".

Playing with family systems as they come alive in the group is serious business and great fun — secrets, triangles, cut-off's, all the relational dynamics and maneuvers get played out right there in front of God and everybody, the only difference being that we learn to name them. And then we can be alert to them and use them to "get in bed" with our patients.

Which reminds me of a beautiful scene in the movie *Wit*, with Emma Thompson as a woman dying of cancer. Her old mentor comes to visit her as she is near death in her hospital bed; the very kindly old lady reads her a children's book, *The Runaway Bunny*, a tender story in which the mother bunny keeps assuring that little bunny that she will always love him. And then, as the dying woman slips toward a coma, the friend climbs into bed with her and holds her. Then it is time for the old friend to get out of bed and leave; the patient is clearly dying. As I have often said to my students, getting in bed with your patient is hard; getting out is just as hard—saying hello and saying goodbye.

Chapter 27

CPE and Church

MORE THAN ONE OF my colleagues in CPE—students and educators—have called the CPE community their church—an apt comparison.

What we love—what gives us life—is found in community.

And, community inevitably develops both formal structures, rules, regulations, and *norms*. In theological language, spirit has to be enfleshed. So each local "church", at a minimum:

- has its own liturgy (even if there is an official "prayer book", it develops its own adaptation of the rites and ceremonies).
- There may be a "designated leader" (perhaps the Educator), but the congregation soon develops its own hierarchy.
- Orthodoxies get developed and challenged.
- There are conflicts, power struggles, personality clashes.
- The Spirit ("God")—acknowledged or not—lives in that congregation. Try as they might, they cannot exclude her, but they can ignore her.
- Evil lives there, too.
- In the midst of all this, they congregate regularly and frequently about the task of living justly, mercifully and humbly with one another, and with the world beyond.

- "God" may be invoked for good or evil or not at all.

Community is what it is all about.

CPE, then, is a crucial educational experience for those who want to be Chaplains in hospitals or other institutional settings; and it is no less crucial for those who want to serve in what has been a more traditional congregational/church setting. People, students, learn what community is by becoming one.

Chapter 28

The Parish Pastor as Chaplain

There may be some who think that Church life, centered around the Parish, as we presently know, it will become obsolete. I suppose that is a possibility, but probably not any time soon.

There was a time when I thought it was somehow a denigration of the parish pastor's role to designate her as *merely* a chaplain to the congregation.

CPE has helped me to a different perspective.

Now my view is that the shape of the pastor's work will be formed in large part by the institution in which he works. But, whatever the setting, the perspective of pastor as chaplain might be understood as the best basic defining perspective—chaplain as the one whose focus is on the Spirit both in the individual and in the community.

And we in ACPE have been about the task for well over half a century of enhancing the pastoral skills, practices and attitudes of ordained (and now, some not ordained, yet otherwise authorized) practitioners of the pastoral care arts—the Chaplain.

It seems to me that there is a long-term drift within ACPE toward a more limited view of Chaplaincy—limited to health care institutions, or more broadly, to other agencies (e.g., prisons, homeless shelters) which are non-Parish church centered. Our literature stresses training for those who will be employed by and serving in such institutions and agencies; it does not, generally, as far as I can tell, stress the importance of providing the same level of training for those who are likely to spend their entire professional lives in service to Parish Churches.

There was an Episcopal Priest named Loren Mead (1930-2018); he became the founding Director of the Alban Institute, an organization whose work was to research parish church life with a view toward making it the life-giving place it could be. He said about his experience of CPE, that the thing that changed his life [in his seminary days in the early 1950's] was clinical training.

I knew Loren slightly and admired his work greatly. His *The Once and Future Church* gives a flavor of his perspective on the possibilities for health-giving life in the life of Parish Churches. Here is how he put it in describing his early work as a Parish Priest in Chapel Hill, North Carolina:

> "I had developed skills as a pretty good counselor, one-to-one. And all of a sudden, I realized Chapel Hill had more good people, counselors, psychiatrists, psychologists, social workers, all kind of people, who really knew how to help people solve their problems. And this town was turning out sick folks faster than we were getting them well. [Laughs] I said, 'Oops, that individual therapy model isn't adequate.' And that's when I made the flip in my mind that what we need a congregation to be is a center of health, spiritual health, all kind of health . . . And to try to infect the community with health, because the things that were going on in the community were basically communicating illness and trouble, but we needed to form a community that was a healing community . . ."

It is, I believe, mostly by historical accident and financial necessity that we have located almost all our CPE Centers in Hospitals—a happy accident, to the benefit of us both.

Our small group work—our attention to systems—means that we practice being a healing community; and that we know the crucial importance of healthy community. We know that physical and spiritual health cannot be separated.

Community means, among other things, mutual support: we need the hospital—it is a marvelous training site; the hospital needs us—we practice the central importance of spirituality to health—the health of individuals and the health of communities.

Chapter 29

Conceptual overreach

This Chapter was originally written as a separate article, inspired by my response to what I deem an oversimplified analysis of a current and significant societal issue. After I had written it, I came across a felicitous phrase from a Professor at Oxford which captured something of what I was concerned about— "conceptual overreach".[1] As I hope is evident by now in these chapters, my conviction is that CPE is at its best when it 'trusts the process' and eschews any rigid outline or schema that purports to provide a comprehensive definition either of 'good' pastoral care practice or its practitioners. So, herewith, a relevant section of that article:

A UNIFIED THEORY OF EVERYTHING

If your map is faulty, you are not likely to get to your desired destination.

I suppose that it is a fairly normal human desire to develop an overarching theory—a map—to account for, to explain, to understand the whole—the terrain—everything. I actually believe in the unity of

1. "All in One", by John Tasioulas, in *Aeon* (an on-line magazine) 1/29/21

everything[2] while at the same time being convinced that that unity is so grand that it is beyond comprehension and can only inspire awe and evoke wonder—and humility. And I acknowledge that each of us has to begin somewhere. Elsewhere in this book I talk about the usefulness as well as the limitations of any one of the many theories about personality and its development, urging students to get familiar with one or more and to beware of being seduced by any of them.

Albert Einstein, and others since, have looked to quantum physics/ mechanics to help develop such a theory. They seem to have come to believe at this point—and note that I intentionally avoid calling it a conclusion—that everything is entangled beyond our capacity to 'understand'; so that, in my simple way of putting it, practically speaking, there is no possibility of a "unified theory".

I recently encountered another angle on the entanglement—the complexity—of human interactions, and the impossibility of any one theory to help us untangle it all, in Samuel Shem's second novel, *Mount Misery*. His novel suggests not only the impossibility, but the actual damage that can be done, in trying to force humanity into one frame. The protagonist, a first year Resident in Psychiatry, is asserting that his current theoretical framework fits his patient perfectly. His wise friend responds, "That's why it's bullshit – *because* it fits. Human beings are so complex, *any* theory fits. By fitting, the theory excludes the complexity, *so you lose what's human.*" [my emphasis here] He goes on to cite, and extrapolate on, Godel's Theorem, in support of the notion there can never be a comprehensive enough theory.[3] Shem's earlier novel, *The House of God*, which I mentioned in Chapter 19, has the wise advisor there ("the fat man") make the same point as he teaches the young interns.

And, from another perspective, philosopher Karl Popper asserts that science never proves anything—and cannot. He affirms the reality of truth, but says that the best any of us can ever do is to approximate our partial grasp of truth *through clear and direct conversation with one another* [my emphasis].

2. See my reference to Dame Julian on p. 79, above.
3. Samuel Shem, *Mount Misery*, page 302

Yet another perspective comes from a brief article in the on-line magazine, *Aeon* (1/18/2121), entitled, "The Mathematical Case Against Blaming People for their Misfortune". The author says,

> "... treating a complex system as though it's simple is a dangerous game; heuristics can misrepresent the world in consequential ways. Indeed, the unpredictability of the course of our lives is partly due to rich causal *complexity of the social world, with its interlocking web of economic, political, psychological and other factors* ... [T]hese conditions of extreme complexity ... are typical of most real-world systems ... "

Once I started attending to this notion, I found references everywhere. For example, I just came upon Albert Murray's book, *The Omni-Americans*, in which he complains of the poverty of much social science writing, of the " ... pretentious terminology and easy oversimplifications [that keep them from remembering] what experience is really like ... they no longer realize how complicated human life is, even at its least troubled and freest ... [and] they are not likely to realize how rich and exciting its possibilities are either."[4]

I cite all those sources above to further emphasize my firm conviction that we humans, each and every one us, are so rich precisely because of our complexity, that we need to be treated with awe, respect, humility and wonder and not as illustrations of a diagnostic category as, for example, in the Psychiatric handbook, DSM (in whichever version it now appears); nor as pawns in any personality theory.

I have some concern that my own beloved ACPE is in danger of falling into the same trap in its insistence on a rigid system of "Objectives and Outcomes".

The beauty and genius of CPE has always been its appreciation for the richness of each person.

---

4. Murray, Albert, *The Omni-Americans*, page 43

Chapter 30

LIFE CONTINUES,
A PERSONAL REFLECTION

I HAD ESSENTIALLY COMPLETED my work on this book before my wife, my life partner for fifty-seven years, died last October. I mean no disrespect here by recalling Mark Twain's comment that when one picks up a cat by the tail, he learns something he can learn in no other way. As a Clergy person and Chaplain, I have been with many people when a person close to them has died. As many of those folks have said, some eloquently and some awkwardly, there are never words adequate to convey what the 'loss' feels like. That doesn't, and shouldn't, deter us from trying to word our grief.

Here's what I wrote to a niece I'm very fond of, and what she wrote back (much more eloquently, I thought) echoing my sentiment as she recalled her mother's death:

> "As for me, I think you know that since Helen died, the size of our apartment and the memories there as well . . . encouraged me to move; and, coincidentally (if there is such a thing) the other side of [daughter] Kate's duplex became available. So I now live next door to her and Alex and Ella. Grief, as you well know, is an odd thing that goes on and on. I miss Helen in all kinds of ways and part of the oddity is that she is both gone and yet still very present in/with me."

And here's what niece, Meredith, said in reply:

> "Grief IS an odd thing. I find as I've gotten older, it's increased
> in some ways (decreased in others) - evolves but doesn't go away
> though there are many times I'm not actively feeling it (and other
> times I am very much feeling it). I've noticed the past few years,
> spring feels like an especially tender time for me (mom's birthday,
> _Mother's Day_, her death anniversary all seem to lump together).
> Different phases of life also bring on different feelings of long-
> ing/missing her. I have a lot of support from friends/family in
> grad school - but sometimes after a crazy day, you just want to
> call your mom and there's no one else who can fill that role. I
> can only imagine the grief of losing someone who you lived with
> and shared your life with for the majority of your years...There's a
> metaphor of walking through "your forest of grief" that somehow
> resonates with me. That part you said about someone is both gone
> and yet still very present also so resonates with me. Death, some-
> times feels abstract - when so much of our knowing of someone is
> done in our heads and our hearts but so much is also the physical
> presence - especially when that person was a daily part of our lives.
> I've learned to remind myself to have conversations with my mom
> in my head. If there isn't a physical person to call, it seems like the
> conversation can't happen, but of course, I have to remind myself
> that isn't entirely true. And sometimes it helps a lot to have those
> head conversations with her. And other days it doesn't and I just
> miss her . . . ."

I still talk to Helen. Once or twice, since she died, I have imagined that
I actually heard her voice calling my name. And much more regularly
I imagine what she would be saying to me in various circumstances.
("Peter! You're not going to wear _that_ are you?") I told my therapist the
other day that I know she's 'gone', but I'm not willing to let her go, totally;
I'm comforted by those recallings. And it is definitely true that it is a
comfort to be able to talk openly about her with friends who knew her.
In an odd way, she remains alive. And that is not denial! I have buried
her ashes at a wonderful funeral service; I know she's dead. But she left
behind many of her beautiful watercolor paintings; she's _in_ them and
so living with me in that and many other ways. And I find myself many
times, feeling/saying, 'What do you think of this, Helen?', followed
sometimes by tears. My friend, Bill Russell, told me about a friend of
his whose wife had died; he told Bill that in the middle of the night he

would reach over in bed to touch her and find an empty space. "Oh, shit", he'd say. Yes.

I irritated a Parishioner years ago when I told him that I always preached what I needed to hear. I guess he thought that was somehow inappropriate. I think many of my clergy friends would agree that that is what we do. Furthermore, I think many would agree that we don't necessarily know that we need to hear it until we hear ourselves saying it. I was once again surprised by a sermon I preached recently, though, in a way, it summarizes my theology pretty completely:

TRINITY CHURCH, CLARKSVILLE

PENTECOST 5, 2021

"It could be said that clergy specialize in making declarations about things we don't know much about and don't understand. That may not be a bad thing; in fact, I'm going to assert that it is a very good thing.

"This week I'm going to venture briefly into a field that I know and understand even less—quantum physics.

"There were some experiments in the early 1900's that seemed to prove that one particle geographically distant from another, with no means of physical contact, could, nevertheless, affect that other. Albert Einstein is supposed to have called it "spooky action at a distance". He didn't like the idea.

"A quantum physicist named Erwin Schroedinger was also troubled by this possibility; he proposed a thought experiment about a cat. Some of you have probably heard about that—a crazy thought experiment: an imagined cat in an imagined box was both dead and alive at the same time. In the strange world of quantum physics both states of being—alive and dead—can coexist in the same time and space, in this thought experiment. Schroedinger's discomfort with the seeming irrationality of quantum theory and particularly what's called the observer effect—that is, it hasn't happened until someone observes it— proposed the cat thought experiment to show the absurdity of quantum theory. He left the field and moved into the study of biology.

"Now don't really worry about all of this; I can promise you that I'm way past my zone of understanding, and I've vastly over-simplified. As the scientist Richard Feynman used to say, "Don't ask how that can be; nobody knows how it can be.""

"What we're talking about here is mystery – mystery.

"You've probably figured out already what it was that got me to thinking along this line:

"We've got two stories in the Gospel for today. Jairus' daughter is dying, and he begs Jesus to come heal her. So as Jesus is on his way, crowded in by a great throng of people, some woman who had suffered for years with bleeding, having heard of Jesus, sneaked up behind him. She figured that all she needed was to touch his robe and she'd be well. You know the story: she touch-es and her body immediately tells her that she is well. Spooky action at a distance. "Who touched me?", he says. "Com'on Je-sus; everybody is touching you". But Jesus stopped and looked around, at which point the woman comes up to him and tells him the whole story. And this is what Jesus says to her, "Your faith has made you well . . . ""

"Just then the message comes from Jairus' house that the girl is dead. "No, she's not"; and they ridiculed him. Once again, Jesus appeals to faith: "Don't be afraid; just believe." And when he gets to the house, he goes into the child's room, takes her hand and says, Get up". And so she does.

"Now I don't believe for a minute that Jesus healed either the woman or the child.

And I'm as sure as I can be that Jesus himself did not think of himself as the one who healed either one of them—or anybody else. He never claimed to be a healer. His message is, "Your faith has made you well".

"The people around him did what the church has been doing ever since: they and we make Jesus into a miracle worker—into something special— different—not like us. We make him into a healer. We make him into something he was not and never claimed to be. There's lots wrong with that understanding of Jesus; we'll get back to that in a minute.

"But, for the moment, here's a thought experiment for us. Picture a child—it might be you—who is in a hard, a scary, situation; (or you might recall the disciples in the boat from last week's story in Mark). The child, the disciples, you are scared. Somebody—your inner voice? Your father? A friend? —somebody you trust says, 'don't be afraid; it's gonna be all right'. And you believe; and it is.

"In essence, Jesus' constant message, over and over again, is "You're afraid, because you don't believe that everything will be all right. I assure you, it will be all right."

"And the people who heard and believed that message, like the woman, found that it was all right.

"Here's what's wrong with making Jesus into God: it relieves us of the responsibility of believing—and declaring—that things will be all right: it is your faith that everything will be all right that will make it so. Making Jesus into God relieves you and me of the responsibility of doing our job: believing, and therefore being, and therefore making it all right.

"Be clear: nothing I'm saying denies that suffering and pain and death are part of life for each and every one.

"So, how can it be that it will be all right? Every time. All right.

"Don't ask how it can be. Nobody knows how it can be.

"The wind goes where it wants to; you hear the sound and see the effects, but you don't know where it comes from or where it goes.

"It is a mystery.

"Therefore, we proclaim the mystery of faith: just believe.

"Healing out of suffering; how can that be?

"A woman whose bleeding stops after twelve years; how can that be?

"Life out of death; how can that be?

"A twelve-year-old lifted from her death bed; how can that be?

"A storm is calmed; how can that be?

"Singer Iris Dement has a wonderful song with the tag line in the refrain,

'I think I'll just let the mystery be'.

"I hope you'll find that song and listen to it.

The good news is simple: trust that it's gonna be all right.

"Don't worry about how: that's a mystery.

"Just know: your faith makes you well."

So I preached that. And then I thought, "As painful as it is to live without Helen living here beside me, as lonely, and lost and 'homeless' as I am right now, *there are moments* when I am *surprised by the certain sense* that it will be all right—I will be all right. I don't know how it and I will be all right, but I know that we will. *There are moments.*

Now, be clear that *it would be pastoral malpractice for the chaplain to rush to assure a grieving family member that everything will be all right.* As I say in the next chapter, such assurance misses the complexity that is an underlying theme in this book. For the moment, death is the reality. But to the extent that the chaplain is coming to terms with "it will be all right" as a conviction she holds for herself as the long-term reality, that conviction may help her stay with the present reality. As Dame Julian of Norwich declared so long ago, "all shall be well", but it may well not yet be the time to say so.

Chapter 31

Toxic Positivity

THE FOLLOWING WAS INITIALLY a separate piece. Yet, following Kierkegaard's notion, the way I have come to understand what I'm thinking is both through hindsight and through writing. I include it here, because it helped me see again, from a fresh perspective, one major learning issue that informs the work of us Clinical Pastoral Educators; and it led to what I believe is perhaps a final maturing of what has been my life-long process of developing a coherent theology.

Back in July, I spent a week at the beach at a wonderful family gathering. I asked the younger folks in the gathering to take the brief survey found in Hans Rosling's book, *Factfulness*.[1] Bright and articulate granddaughter, Ellis, had an immediate and strongly negative response about the book. There wasn't opportunity at that moment to explore her reaction, but later she was gracious to explain that she had heard enough about the book to fear that it was promoting what she called 'toxic positivity'.

I had never even heard that term. Google affirms that there was such a thing and described it as a mode of denial, a false assurance. One defining statement noted that "Toxic positivity is *an obsession with positive thinking*. It is the belief that people should put a positive spin on all experiences, even those that are profoundly tragic. Examples offered: "look on the bright side" or "everything happens for a reason", or (a particularly cruel one), "you can have another baby".

1. Rosling, Hans, *Factfulness*

I thanked Ellis for explaining; her concern makes perfect sense. It took me a while to recognize that she had given me new name for what is one of the major learning issues in CPE. Students are typically tempted to offer an easy assurance ("It's all right"; "God is with you". "God doesn't lay on us more than we can bear . . . ")—"toxic positivity" indeed! It is part of my task to help them see that they are thus avoiding feeling the pain that is so vividly present in the one suffering: this is the pain that *the Pastor—that she herself*—will have to *live into and feel—with her patient* [which is what compassion means]—if she if she stays in the room and doesn't allow herself to escape to the "positive". In essence, what I hope and believe all my students must learn is that no one can skip a step; if there is any hope, it is in living each part of life fully as it comes along. "Weeping spends the night".[2] So must the Chaplain.

Rosling absolutely agrees with Ellis's concern:

> "My guess is you *feel* that me saying that the world is getting better is like me telling you that everything is fine, or that you should . . . pretend the problems don't exist . . . I agree. Everything is not fine . . . as long as there are [here Rosling gives a long list of real and significant problems], as long as such things exist, we cannot relax. But, [Rosling adds] it is just as ridiculous, and just as stressful to look away from the progress that has been made."

Rosling eschews the appellation "optimist" for himself; "I'm a very serious "possibilist" . . . someone who neither hopes without reason, nor fears without reason, someone who constantly resists the overdramatic worldview."[3]

Rosling accomplishes two things in writing this book: one is to provide hard data documenting the various improvements in our world over time; the other is to address the various ways that we are blind to those accomplishments and to some of *the negative consequences of our misperceiving (e.g., a tendency to unwarranted pessimism and a tendency to overreact by ill-conceived "remedies").*

Elaine Pagels, in her book, *Why Religion?*[4], raises the same concern as Ellis does, only more pointedly aimed at Christianity: she decries " . . .

---

2. Psalm 30:5. (See my comment about this in the preface.)

3. Rosling, pp.68-69

4. Pagels, *Why Religion*, pp. 168-169

the facile comfort that churches often dole out like Kleenex". And to make her point, as a Biblical scholar she references the Gospel of Mark and notes that the original ending of that book is decidedly an unhappy one:

> "In the original version that Mark wrote, Jesus, crucified in agony, cries out '*My God, my God, why have you abandoned me?*', then lets out a loud cry and dies. Similar things have happened, of course, to countless others, and still do. And in Mark's original version, as so often in stories we hear today, no angel appears, no miracle intervenes. Instead . . . this story ends with an abrupt, disturbing scene at the gravesite . . . [the body is missing] . . . So far as we can tell . . . someone among Mark's early readers, wanting the Gospel to end on a more positive note, wrote a *second* ending . . . "

And that, simply, is also my objection to what the Church has done with the Jesus story. Like the one who, arguably, added the happy ending to Job, someone added a happy ending to Mark. We can't stand the harsh truth that death is the end. We often add our own happy ending.

We rush to the third day, and we tell one another that the empty tomb means resurrection—Jesus is alive!

NO!

Jesus is dead.

To the extent that we can say that Jesus means to re-present God, the only reasonable conclusion is that in God's world the conclusion to each life is that it ends in death. Jesus models accepting that reality.

Maybe the proper response is to do what Jesus did at his friend Lazarus' death: "Jesus wept"[5].

"Is that all there is?" you might ask. "Weep?"[6]

I guess the only way you can find out if there is more . . . is to weep.

---

5. John 11:35
6. Peggy Lee comes to mind

Chapter 32

Some More Acknowledgements and a Concluding Story

Years ago, a parishioner gave me a small framed saying of Michelangelo. On the day of his death, my parishioner told me, Michelangelo said, "I am still learning".

I have been extraordinarily fortunate in having been given so many opportunities to learn. "Given" is the operative word. People often ask for the definition of "grace". It can't be defined.[1] But something of its sense can be captured in discovering how much is out there—*given to us*: richness, beauty, pain, suffering, people, animals, life, death; *and* the ability to perceive them, feel them, think them—experience them and learn (grow). My life has been graced with lots of gifts.

Specific instances: my very gifted artist wife who never gave up trying to help me slow down, observe, and appreciate all the beauty around me. Two remarkably thoughtful children and eight grandchildren—I'm still coming to appreciate them and all that they are advertantly [is there such a word?] and inadvertently teaching me. Parishioners, counselees,

1. There's a great little story, surely apocryphal, about the northerner traveling in the south who went to a restaurant in a small southern town for breakfast. He gave the waitress his order and added, emphatically, "No Grits! I don't want any grits". She brought his order, and sure enough, there on the plate were grits. He protested. And, in her gentle, sweet southern way she said, "Honey, grits is like grace; you get it whether you want it or not."

111

students, peers, clergy colleagues—rich, diverse, willing to open themselves in trusting friendship.

Helen left me recently. I dedicate this book to her, with the following brief story:

THE SWEATER

"You're next", she said, guiding me to her barber chair.

"I'm Heather; I hope you are having a nice day".

I responded in kind. Then there was some discussion about how I wanted my hair cut.

"That is a pretty sweater", she said.

"Thank you", I said.

It is so rare as to be almost unknown that I would share any personal stories with a stranger. I don't know what moved me to continue.

"I'll tell you a story about this sweater, a little sad and a little happy.

"My wife died very recently, that's the sadness."

"Mmmm", she agreed.

"But here's the other part: first, you need to know that there was a sort of joke between us. One time, some years ago, she told me she planned to give me a sweater for Christmas. 'But Helen, I already *have* a sweater(!)', I told her. She has loved telling friends and teasing me about that response.

"Shortly after my wife died a woman who had become a good friend to us both came by our apartment with a gift wrapped in Christmas paper. She and other close friends had been very kind to me since Helen died; but a Christmas present in the middle of November seemed a little peculiar. 'You can open it now or wait until Christmas', she said. Of course, you know what I did."

Heather agreed that she understood that I opened it immediately.

"In the box was this sweater—and a note.

"Now you also need to know that this friend loved catalogues at least as much as Helen did. We would sometimes get four or five catalogues delivered by our postman in one day; likewise, our friend. And she and Helen loved to peruse and discuss the endless possibilities offered in those catalogues. And after Helen died, and those catalogues continued their avalanche, I had declared that I was going to cancel every one of those damn catalogues!

"This is what the friend's note said, 'Dear Peter, before you *completely abolish* Helen's catalogues, you need a reminder that lots of good come from them. Long ago, back in late Spring, Helen and I conspired on your Christmas gift. She asked me to order it for you, then asked me to charge it, have it delivered, and stored at [my] residence! All this was despite the fact that when she asked you for some money, you kept wanting to know what she needed the money for. Finally she told you it was none of your business and added, 'Just give me the damn money!'. The wrapping was *mine*, but the heart (and the money!) was Helen's. Just so you know . . . '

"Isn't that a nice story?"

I got a little teary. I think Heather did, too.

Grace abounding.

BIBLIOGRAPHY

Gleick, James, *Genius*, New York, Pantheon Books, 1992

De Mello, Anthony, S.J. *One Minute Nonsense*, Chicago, Loyola Press, 1992

————. *More One Minute Nonsense*, Chicago, Loyola Press, 1999

De Vries, Peter, *The Blood of the Lamb*, Little, Brown & Company, 1961

Friedman, Ed, *Generation to Generation: Family Process in Church and Synagogue*, Guiford, 2011

Healy, Nan Savage, *Toni Wolff & C.G. Jung*, Los Angeles, TiberiusPress, 2017

Hillsman, Gordon, *How To Get the Most Out of Clinical Pastoral Education: A CPE Primer*, Jessica Kingsley, Publisher

Keese, Peter, *Jesus Has Left the Building*, Eugene, Oregon, Wipf and Stock, Publishers, 2014

Malone, Michael, *Handling Sin*, Boston, Little, Brown and Company, 1984

Madden, Myron, *The Power to Bless*, Chicago, Insight Press, Inc, revised edition, 1999

McFague, Sallie, *Metaphorical Theology: Models of God on Religious Language*, Philadelphia, Fortress Press, 1982

Mead, Loren, *The Once and Future Church*, Washington, Alban Institute, Inc., 1991

Murray, Albert, *The Omni-Americans*, Library of America, 1970

Napier, Augustus and Whitaker, Carl, *Family Crucible*, Harper Collins, 1978

Pagels, Elaine, *Why Religion?*, New York, Harper Collins, 2018

Rosling, Hans, *Factfulness*, New York, Flatiron Books, 2018

Shem, Samuel, *The House of God*, New York, Bantam Dell, Random House, Inc, 1978

————. *Mount Misery*, New York, Bantam Dell, Random House, 1981

Yalom, Irvin & Elkin, Ginny, *Every Day Gets a Little Closer*, New York, Basic Books, Inc., 1974

Yalom, Irvin, *Love's Executioner*, New York, Basic Books, Inc, 1989

Made in the USA
Columbia, SC
15 March 2022

57712660R10075